52 WEEKS OF
Wow
FAITH

Hope and Encouragement for Tough Times

Mary E. Banks

Mobile, Alabama

52 Weeks of WOW Faith
by Mary E. Banks
Copyright ©2009 Mary E. Banks

All rights reserved. This book is protected under the copyright laws of the United States of America. This book may not be copied or reprinted for commercial gain or profit. Unless otherwise identified, Scripture quotations are taken from the *Holy Bible, New Living Translation,* copyright ©1996. Used by permission of Tyndale House Publishers, Inc., Wheaton, Illinois 60189. All rights reserved.

Scriptures marked HCSB are taken from the *Comparative Study Bible, Revised Edition,* copyright ©1999 by The Zondervan Corporation.

Scriptures marked AMP are taken from the *Amplified Bible, Expanded Edition,* copyright ©1987 by the Zondervan Corporation and the Lockman Foundation.

Scriptures marked NIV are taken from the *Holy Bible, New International Version*, copyright ©1973, 1978, 1984 by the International Bible Society.

Scriptures marked MSG are taken from *The Message: The Bible in contemporary language* ©2002 by Eugene H. Peterson.

Scriptures marked NKJV are taken from the *New King James Version,* copyright ©1982 by Thomas Nelson, Inc.

ISBN 978-1-58169-320-1
For Worldwide Distribution
Printed in the U.S.A.

Evergreen Press
P.O. Box 191540 • Mobile, AL 36619
800-367-8203
www.evergreenpress.com

DEDICATION

To my darling daughter, Elise Nicole.

Being your mother has been the supreme joy of my life! So much of what is written between these covers was inspired by you. Thanks for allowing God to use your life to teach me about His great love and for always keeping it real.

Acknowledgments

It is a joyful task to express gratitude to those whose ideas and lives have helped shape this book's message. Foremost is Beth Moore, through whose ministry I learned the simplicity and the power of the Gospel and the joy of not only believing in God but believing God. I am also grateful for the ministry of Bible Study Fellowship. It is through this ministry that I realized the importance of staying in the Word of God daily as a way of life. I also wish to thank all those faithful writers whose books and articles have taught me the beauty of the written word and filled my life with endless wonder, challenged my thinking and taken me to places I may never have the opportunity to visit but can see clearly in my mind because of their talented writing and excellent use of word pictures.

I wish to thank my family and friends for always encouraging me to keep writing. They say ridiculous things like, "I just love the way you write" and "you are such a gifted writer," which convinces me that they have terrible taste in writers but thrills my heart just the same and only inspires me to get better at something I absolutely adore doing.

It is an honor to have as my publisher, Brian Banashak and the entire team at Evergreen Press. He is a man of integrity and welcomed this book project with enthusiasm from the beginning. Many thanks to Kathy Banashak, the senior editor for this book—she has such a servant's heart and I greatly appreciate that. I am also grateful to those who read the manuscript and generously agreed to endorse it. Thank you for sharing your good name with me.

The deepest gratitude is always to my family. My husband, Melvin, whose unflagging support for my work, means the world to me. To my daughter, Elise, who allows me to use her (and even her friends) in many of my stories and has provided me with book content for years to come. To my parents, my sisters and brother, and my mother-in-law, all of whom have shaped my life in such a special and unique way. I am a blessed woman to have all of these amazing people in my life!

Finally, I want to thank the Lord God our Creator. It would take pages and pages covering the entire earth and then some, to tell of Your glory. This book doesn't even begin to scratch the surface of who You are, but I offer it as a sacrifice of praise.

Mary E. Banks
April 20, 2009

TABLE OF CONTENTS

Introduction		vii
Week 1:	A New Perspective	1
Week 2:	A Call to Battle	3
Week 3:	Purpose	5
Week 4:	Growing Wiser	8
Week 5:	Adversity—A Call to Action	10
Week 6:	Doing God's Work God's Way	13
Week 7:	Doing the Small Things	16
Week 8:	Releasing What You Hold Dear	19
Week 9:	Enduring the Wait	23
Week 10:	Running Your Race	26
Week 11:	In the Fire With God	29
Week 12:	Developing a Habit of Thanks	32
Week 13:	Waiting on God's Timing	35
Week 14:	God's Passion	38
Week 15:	Walking in Your Gethsemane	40
Week 16:	The Gift of Pain	42
Week 17:	Confidence During the Storm	45
Week 18:	The Temptation to Compromise	48
Week 19:	Standing Firm Against Fear	51
Week 20:	God's Dream for Us	54
Week 21:	Help for Life's Giants	57
Week 22:	God's Busy Schedule	60
Week 23:	Are You Speaking Blessings?	62
Week 24:	God's Special Secrets for You!	65
Week 25:	Divine Plans for You!	68
Week 26:	How You See Yourself Matters!	71
Week 27:	Sowing and Reaping	74
Week 28:	Choose To Be Content	76

Week 29:	Waiting on Something New	79
Week 30:	Is It Raining in Someone's Life?	82
Week 31:	Walking by Faith	85
Week 32:	The Truth About Who You Are	88
Week 33:	God Can Do What Even Oprah Can't	92
Week 34:	No More Window Shopping	95
Week 35:	Have You Lost Your Way?	98
Week 36:	Your Rainbow of Hope	101
Week 37:	Time in God's Waiting Room	104
Week 38:	God Wants Us To Win!	107
Week 39:	Praying for Our Children	110
Week 40:	Are You Waiting on an Answer or Waiting on God?	113
Week 41:	The Blessings of Lingering	116
Week 42:	Struggling To Obey	120
Week 43:	Destinations	124
Week 44:	Are You Living Greatly?	127
Week 45:	A Homecoming	130
Week 46:	I've Got You Covered!	132
Week 47:	What Season Is It Now?	135
Week 48:	Praise After the Storm	137
Week 49:	Second Chances	139
Week 50:	What Would You Do If You Really Believed God?	142
Week 51:	A Better Vantage Point	145
Week 52:	The Challenge	147

INTRODUCTION

"Blessing is bowing down to receive the expressions of divine favor that in the inner recesses of the human heart make life worth the bother," Beth Moore said in her powerful daily devotional *Believing God*. Moore defines blessing as so much more than an easy life, getting a great parking spot at the mall, or being upgraded to a better seat on an airplane. She asks, "Would we know His blessing if we saw it?" This caused me to wonder if I would.

As I began writing this devotional, I couldn't help but realize how blessed my life has been in so many profound ways. The fact that I have an eternal hope still amazes me. From an early age, my pursuit of God began. I can't remember when I didn't want to know Him. As a young child, I thought He was my mother's imaginary friend. My mother talked to Him in hushed whispers as she worked around the house. It seemed as though she couldn't wait to spend time with Him, and I often saw her in her favorite quiet place to read "His Words" as though it was a long letter from a dear old friend. I often caught her staring into the heavenlies at prayer time as though she could really see His face.

Oh yes, she had piqued the interest of my tiny heart, and I wanted so much to know Him—to have an introduction to my mother's great Friend. And so my pursuit began. I looked for Him in the chalice of my Catholic church and searched for Him in the confessional behind the screen where only the priests could go. In later years, I sought Him through the crusades of the great Dr. Billy Graham. I often questioned my mother, "Why didn't He call on ten thousand angels rather than die that awful death on a tree? Wasn't He a friend of God? Wouldn't God have come?"

I now realize that He didn't call the angels because He was pursuing me! Before I was born, before I knew to want Him or seek Him, He was seeking me. He was showing up in all those places, gently knocking on the door to my heart saying, "Here I am child, right here."

So when I think of blessing, I must start with the miracle of awareness—the awareness of who He is and the awareness of the pursuit that I thought began with me but I now realize began with Him. Only He could have placed in me the capability to believe this truth. My belief is not merely in some higher power, nor that God merely exists. The fact that I believe in a personal, intimate, interested, involved, loving, pursuing God **is** the blessing. All other blessings originate from this blessing. So the question, "Would we know His blessing if we saw it?" can be answered fairly simply in the negative—at least not at first. As a result, a mission began taking shape in my heart. The mission was to encourage the hearts of others as they journeyed to find God too. Realizing that our own personal filters cause us to focus on all the wrong things, I knew that others might need a little help on their journeys in the same way that my mother had helped me.

And that is how the idea for this devotional took shape. I have decided the greatest blessing is the difference between the words *by* and *with*. We need to understand the difference between being blessed *by* God and being blessed *with* God Himself. I hope that those reading this devotional will discover the blessing of His presence in good times and bad times. I believe God wants us to know Him even in the mundane details of life. This book is designed to provide you with an opportunity to reflect on who God is and to realize that He is in pursuit of you.

In order to get the most benefit from this devotional, have your Bible, prayer journal, and a pen ready. The devotional is divided into fifty-two weeks—one devotional reading for each week of the year. Each devotional also has six questions at the conclusion of the chapter. This will provide you with the opportunity to have a daily question to meditate upon, consider, and answer. On the seventh day, you may journal what you believe God has taught you as a result of the devotional reading.

I am praying that this devotional book will encourage you, bless you, and help you to grow into the woman or man of God you are designed to be. But most importantly, I am praying that the God of all comfort and hope will make Himself real to you and will be glorified in every page, and that you will come to know Him as you never have before.

⇝ Week 1: A New Perspective ⇜

A new year arrives, and everything starts fresh. Even when you're in the middle of something, it's as though a new perspective is available when a new year begins.

Today as I was beginning my quiet time, I thought about how pleasant it was to begin the day just enjoying God's presence. I began to sing a song of praise, and as I did, the sun broke through the clouds for just a moment. It was surprising to see the sun because the weather has been cloudy and rainy the past couple of days. Oddly enough, the day was still very cloudy as though it would rain at any moment. And yet the sun seemed to be saying, "I just want you to know despite how it seems, I'm still here!" After making that brief appearance, the sun disappeared again. I continued to stare at the place in the sky where it had been, and then I smiled as I realized that I had just had a "God moment."

Oh, how like life it is that when our world is sunny and bright, and circumstances are working just the way we want them to, we can see God in everything. But when life becomes gloomy and overcast, when our circumstances are difficult or even fearful, we wonder if God has abandoned us. Like the sun, at those times God may send us little reminders of His presence. It may be through words of encouragement from a friend or though the kindness of a stranger. We can't see Him or feel Him during those cloudy days; but through those God moments, He is saying, "I just want you to know, despite how it seems, I'm still here!"

He is ever faithful, ever present, and we come to know suddenly that His Word is true, *"When you pass through the waters, I will be with you"* (Isaiah 42:2).

The next time circumstances have you wondering where God is, remember the lesson we learn from nature and grab a new perspective. We may not see the sun behind the clouds, but it is there. And, dear friend, so is God.

Week 1 Memory Verse

When you pass through the waters, I will be with you (Isaiah 42:2 AMP).

Daily Quiet Reflections

Has God ever given you an experience that helped you to keep your life in perspective? Describe one of these experiences.
_____
_____

How have these experiences equipped you to trust God for your future?
_____
_____

What is your first reaction when God is not responding the way you want Him to in the trials of your life?
_____
_____

How have these trials increased your maturity in Christ?
_____
_____

What are some ways you can grow in this area of your life?
_____
_____

What is the promise that God gives in Isaiah 42:2? How does this truth impact your life today?
_____
_____

⇾ Week 2: A Call to Battle ⇽

The Lord left certain nations in the land to test those Israelites who had not participated in the wars of Canaan. He did this to teach warfare to generations of Israelites who had no experience in battle (Judges 3:1–2).

Has the Lord allowed something to remain in your life to teach you how to enter into spiritual warfare? Has He permitted some circumstance or a relationship to continue in your life so that you grow in the techniques of true spiritual battle?

In the passage above, Moses and Joshua, the great leaders of the children of Israel, were already dead. Many of the warriors that had fought with Joshua to claim the land of Canaan were also dead. What was left behind was a generation of people who had no experience in warfare. And the passage says that God left certain nations in the land that was to belong to the children of Israel so that He could teach them how to be effective in battle.

I am reminded of a time when I had no spiritual fighting skills. The enemy would come against me and knock me over, and I would sit up thinking, *What happened?* It doesn't take long to get sick and tired of being knocked over before you cry out, "Lord what am I to learn from this situation? How do I gain the victory in my life?" It is during our crying out times that we begin to inch closer to God, looking to Him for direction and instruction. This is exactly what He wants us to do. He says, *"How good it is to be near God"* (Psalm 73:28). It is during this time with the Lord that we learn how to fight the good fight of faith. It is while we are drawing near to God that our spiritual muscles begin to grow, and the skills that we need to have victory in our lives is developed.

The next time you find yourself wondering, *Why is this happening to me?* remember that God may be using this as a time to bring you closer to Him through the reading of His Word and fellowship with Him through prayer. Challenges will also strengthen your spiritual muscles. Always know that He promises to *"rescue those who love Him"* (Psalm 91:14).

Week 2 Memory Verse

. . . It is not by force nor by strength, but by my Spirit, says the Lord of Heaven's Armies (Zechariah 4:6).

Daily Quiet Reflections

When was the last time God allowed something to remain in your life to teach you how to enter into spiritual warfare?
___
___

What did you learn from that experience?
___
___

What do you think is meant by this week's memory verse, "not by force nor by strength, but by my Spirit"?
___
___

How can memorizing this Scripture help you to remain focused on the true nature of spiritual warfare?
___
___

Read Judges 4:4-23. What is the difference between how Deborah handles her circumstances and how Barak deals with the very same set of circumstances? How can you apply the lessons from Deborah's story to your own life?
___
___

Write a prayer of thanks to the Lord for the circumstances that have taught you to develop your spiritual muscles.
___
___

⇸ Week 3: Purpose ⇷

Have you ever asked the question, *For what purpose was I created?* or *When God thought about me, what exactly did He intend for me to do here on earth?*

There is an interesting story in the Bible that tells about John the Baptist and his purpose. In this narrative, we find him already in ministry and being questioned by the Jewish priest and leaders. John 1:19-24 describes the scene. The leaders are trying to determine if John is the Messiah for whom they have been waiting. When he tells them he is not, they ask if he is Elijah or a prophet, which he also denies. Finally, in frustration they ask, "Who are you?" He answers by quoting the prophet Isaiah, *"I am a voice shouting in the wilderness. Prepare a straight pathway for the Lord's coming"* (Isaiah 40:3).

I have often wondered about this passage. It is obvious that John was very clear about his purpose in life. He knew what he was born to do. Do you have this same certainty of knowing your purpose? Are you really sure, without a doubt, why you were created? If not, you may wonder as I did, *How was John so sure? How did he really know that he was the person Isaiah had prophesied would eventually come? How did He know that it was for this purpose that he had been born?* Especially when we are in the midst of trials that seem endless, we often question our purpose. We need to see how what we are experiencing fits into God's plan for our lives; otherwise, our hope can fade.

In Luke 1:29-38, John reveals the intimacy of his relationship with God. He describes how he was able to recognize that Jesus was the Son of God and says, "I didn't know He was the one, but when God sent me to baptize with water He told me, 'When you see the Holy Spirit descending and resting upon someone, He is the one you are looking for. He is the one who baptizes with the Holy Spirit.' John said, "I saw this happen to Jesus, so I testify that He is the Son of God." Notice those key words, "He told me." It is obvious that John had the type of relationship with God that suggests a great closeness—how else would he have recognized the voice of God in this matter? It would stand to reason that if God told him whom to watch for, He also told him that his purpose was to watch. While watching, he was to alert others to the Messiah's impending arrival! Clearly, John knew his purpose because God told him what it was!

Is it possible for us to have that same certainty? Of course! The Bible teaches that God is not a respecter of persons. In other words, He doesn't have favorites among His children. He wants us to know why we were created. He wants us to be as certain of our purposes in life as John the Baptist was of his.

Don't be afraid to ask God to reveal His design for your life. Spend time with Him so that you learn to recognize the gentle sound of his voice as He directs you through the Scriptures to your amazing purpose. Believe me, your hope will increase and the present tough times will not seem as difficult. It will make facing your existing challenges much easier.

Week 3 Memory Verse

If you need wisdom, ask our generous God, and he will give it to you. He will not rebuke you for asking (James 1:5).

Daily Quiet Reflections

Think back to a time when you felt content, happy, peaceful, and fulfilled. What was it about that time that generated a sense of purpose?

_____

_____

What are your three greatest values?

_____

_____

How do you express your purpose through your values?

_____

_____

What is the biggest barrier in perceiving and understanding your purpose?

_____

_____

If you were to describe your purpose for being, how would you define it?

_____

_____

What is the most significant action you can take today to move closer to your purpose?

_____

_____

☙ Week 4: Growing Wiser ❧

As Samuel grew up, the Lord was with him, and everything Samuel said was wise and helpful (I Samuel 3:19).

Are you growing wiser and more helpful as you grow in your knowledge of God? Samuel was a man who had been dedicated for service to God by his parents at a young age. He studied under Eli the prophet and learned to hear the voice of God.

We are also required to learn to hear God's voice in our lives. In order to grow in our faith, we must discipline ourselves to read the Word of God daily and then apply what we read to our lives.

As we grow up in our faith, we should also grow in wisdom, and our words should be of help to others. There are many people who have great knowledge of God's Word but never take the time to apply it to their lives or use it as a way to encourage others. You might feel as if you are the only one experiencing difficulties; but if you look around, you will see that there are many more people going through tough times. You can help encourage them by sharing how God has brought you through trials in your life. As you find an encouraging verse, you might even share this with them in an email.

Make it a daily priority to grow up in your faith. Say to yourself, *I will spend time in God's Word every day*. And then do it! But more importantly, ask God to show you ways to apply His Word and to give you opportunities to encourage and help others in all that you say. As you do this, you will feel God's presence in your life, and like Samuel, everything you say will be wise and helpful to those whom God places in your life.

Week 4 Memory Verse

For the word of God is alive and powerful. It is sharper than the sharpest two-edged sword, cutting between soul and spirit, between joint and marrow. It exposes our innermost thoughts and desires (Hebrews 4:12).

Daily Quiet Reflections

Based on this week's memory verse, why do you think knowing God's Word is important for developing wisdom?
_____
_____

The Bible says, *"King Solomon became richer and wiser than any other king in all the earth"* (2 Chronicles 9:22). Read 2 Chronicles 1:1-12. What did Solomon request of God, and how did God respond to his request?
_____
_____

What can you learn from Solomon's example?
_____
_____

Read Proverbs 8. What are some of the key benefits of wisdom?
_____
_____

What hinders you from spending time in God's Word daily?
_____
_____

Pray and ask God to instill in you a desire to spend time daily in His Word.

⇝ Week 5: Adversity—A Call to Action ⇜

Saul was one of the official witnesses at the killing of Stephen. A great wave of persecution began that day, sweeping over the church in Jerusalem, and all the believers except the apostles fled into Judea and Samaria. Some godly men came and buried Stephen with loud weeping. Saul was going everywhere to devastate the church. He went from house to house, dragging out both men and women to throw them into jail. But the believers who had fled Jerusalem went everywhere preaching the good news about Jesus. Phillip, for example, went to the city of Samaria and told the people there about the Messiah. Crowds listened intently to what he had to say because of the miracles he did (Acts 8:1-6).

I am always amazed at the unique ways that God uses to move His people in the direction that He wants them to go. Sometimes He uses adversity. As much as we dislike having unpleasant situations in our lives, that is when we become more prone to act. For example, in the passage of Scripture above, we see the beginnings of the persecution of the church. Up until that time, the believers in Jesus had been enjoying a time of fellowship and rejoicing that the Messiah had indeed come just as God promised. Yes, there had been some problems with the local religious leaders; and after the death of Stephen, the persecution of the believers had intensified. As a result, many of them fled Jerusalem.

But as they fled, they begin preaching the good news to others in distant places! Isn't it so like God to use adversity to help His children move in the direction they need to go? God's desire was for the new believers to spread the word about Jesus. Had He not allowed this adversity into their lives, they may have settled for staying where they were. Instead, it was the adversity that compelled them to go and tell people elsewhere about the good news of Christ.

Have you found yourself in a similar situation today? Was life going along as normal, and then suddenly chaos struck? Is there some adversity in your life that may exist to help you move out of your comfort zone and into God's greater plan for your life? God tells us to be truly glad, explaining, *"There is wonderful joy ahead even though it is necessary for you to endure many trials for a while. These trials are only to test your faith, to show that it is strong and pure"* (1 Peter 1:6-7).

When God allows adversity in our lives, He still has a good plan in mind. Not only will it be a plan to bless us, but it will also be a plan to bless others.

So hang tough! Trust God! This adversity didn't come to stay; it came to pass!

Week 5 Memory Verse

When troubles come your way, consider it an opportunity for great joy. For you know that when your faith is tested, your endurance has a chance to grow. So let it grow, for when your endurance is fully developed, you will be perfect and complete, needing nothing (James 1:2-4).

Daily Quiet Reflections

What have been some key lessons that you have learned while going through a time of adversity?
_____
_____

How have these lessons helped you in your faith walk?
_____
_____

What is one way that you can maintain your joy even in difficult circumstances?
_____
_____

What role does the Holy Spirit play in helping you to endure tests of faith?
_____
_____

Is there any action that God may want you to take as a result of some adversity in your life? If so, what do you think He is calling you to do?
_____
_____

Pray and ask God to provide endurance during a time of adversity so that you may be complete, needing nothing.

↣ Week 6: Doing God's Work God's Way ↢

Have you ever had a difficult task to do and weren't sure how to complete it or were uncertain if you had the skills to do so? That is the situation in which King Solomon found himself. Solomon had the responsibility of building the temple of the Lord. It was a massive undertaking that required thousands of pounds of materials, hundreds of laborers, and the ability to pay close attention to details. Imagine the pressure Solomon must have felt at the importance of this great task—building the temple of the Lord.

Solomon had many perceived strikes against him. First, he was very young. Second, he lacked experience. Third, a project of this magnitude had never been done before, so he had no example to follow.

How many times have we found ourselves in that place? Some seemingly impossible task or situation has been given to us to deal with, and we are full of all the reasons why we may not be up to the task. We may lack the experience or possibly the resources that we think we need. Maybe we are young and have no example to follow. Or in some cases, we simply lack the confidence that we can get it done.

Well, there is encouragement from God's Word when we find ourselves in over our heads. And it comes from the words of King David as he encouraged his son, Solomon, in his great task:

Be strong and courageous, and do the work. Don't be afraid or discouraged by the size of the task, for the Lord God, my God, is with you. He will not fail you or forsake you. He will see to it that all the work related to the temple of the Lord is finished correctly (1 Chronicles 28:20).

This brings up a very important precept. When the Lord gives us a task, He will make sure we have what we need to complete it successfully. The key to our success in any difficult task is to plug in to

God's amazing power. If it is His work, then He will make sure that it gets finished. So, how do we plug in to God's power? More wise counsel comes from King David to Solomon,

> *Get to know the God of your ancestors. Worship and serve him with your whole heart and with a willing mind. For the Lord sees every heart and understands and knows every plan and thought. If you seek him, you will find him* (1 Chronicles 28:9).

When facing a difficult task, seek God. Ask Him to show you how to start and how to finish the task. You have His assurance that when you seek Him, He will make Himself available to you. What may have appeared to be impossible to you becomes very small when placed in the hands of our amazing God!

Week 6 Memory Verse

Jesus looked at them intently and said, "Humanly speaking, it is impossible. But not with God. Everything is possible with God" (Mark 10:27).

Daily Quiet Reflections

What have been some tasks that you were faced with that were difficult for you to accomplish?

_____
_____

During those times, has it been your practice to ask God for His help? If not, why not?

_____
_____

Our culture teaches us to be self-sufficient. How is this mindset counter to what God wants for us?

_____
_____

What do you gain by learning to ask for God's help when you are faced with a difficult task?

_____
_____

Ask yourself, *What would I do if I were not afraid?* List all the actions you would take to move forward in your difficult task if fear wasn't there to hinder you.

_____
_____

Take your list to God in prayer and ask for His assistance in undertakings that will bring Him glory.

→ Week 7: Doing the Small Things ←

Have you always desired to do a great work for God, only to have Him respond by asking you to do a small work? Has He instructed you to do something so small that you considered it insignificant and not important enough? That is how Naaman felt.

Naaman was a mighty warrior and the commander of the armies of King Aram. The king had great respect for Naaman because they had won many battles through his leadership and skill. But the Bible says that Naaman suffered from leprosy (2 Kings 5:9-14), a very serious skin disease which hampered his life significantly. Naaman found out that there was a prophet in Israel, named Elisha, who served God and could perform healing miracles. King Aram was told about this, and he gave Naaman permission to go to the king of Israel and request that he be healed.

One thing led to another, and Naaman found himself at the door of Elisha's home after traveling a far distance. However, Elisha did not come out to see Naaman. Instead, he sent a messenger out to Naaman and instructed him to go and wash himself seven times in the Jordan River. He was assured that he would be healed of leprosy if he did this.

Naaman was furious and stalked away! He had expected Elisha to come out and call on God in some dramatic fashion to restore his health. He ranted about what Elisha had asked him to do and refused to do it. Naaman was fortunate to have some of his officers with him who attempted to reason with him. They said, *"Sir, if the prophet had told you to do some great thing, wouldn't you have done it? So you should certainly obey him when he says simply to go and wash and be cured!"* (2 Kings 5:13). As a result, Naaman followed their counsel, went to the Jordan River, washed himself, and was cured!

How many times have we responded as Naaman did when asked to do a small task for the Lord? All of us have a tendency to want to do what we perceive as great exploits for God because of our love for Him and our sincere desire to honor Him. If He asked us to run a church project or be in charge of a highly visible fundraiser, we would jump at the opportunity, eager to serve God in such a noticeable fashion. But what about the times He has asked us to serve Him by cleaning up after an event or by serving in the nursery at church, rocking crying babies? Are we equally as willing to serve Him in these small matters noticed only by Him? Imagine what blessings we may have missed because we chose not to obey God in the small matters.

Let us not respond as Naaman initially did when he was called to what he perceived as a small task. He was literally one bath away from a miracle! It was a trifling deed to do, and he almost missed his miracle due to his pride. Who knows? Today you may be "one bath" away from your miracle too! God may have called you to a seemingly insignificant responsibility. But it is when we are obedient to God in the small assignments that we begin to see His daily miracles in our lives.

Obeying God by joyfully performing the small tasks of life creates a desire in God to perform great and mighty miracles on our behalf. So the next time God gives you something small to do—just do it!

Week 7 Memory Verse

The master was full of praise. "Well done, my good and faithful servant. You have been faithful in handling this small amount, so now I will give you many more responsibilities. Let's celebrate together!" (Matthew 25:21)

Daily Quiet Reflections

List some of the small responsibilities that God may have placed in your life right now. Why may God see them as your most important duties during this season of your life?
___
___

Read the story of the faithful servant in Matthew 25:14-30. What does this lesson teach you about the appropriate use of your talents?
___
___

What are some of the excuses you have used to avoid doing the tasks God is calling you to do?
___
___

What role has self-centeredness played in keeping you from being motivated to do what is considered small in your eyes?
___
___

What is one of the key ways that God rewards those who are faithful to the task at hand?
___
___

Identify what you can do today to make God's priorities your priorities, no matter how small they may appear to you.
___
___

↣ Week 8: Releasing What You Hold Dear ↢

Sometimes we are afraid to let go of our most precious possessions because we believe that if we do, all is lost. In other words, we don't like losing control. This precious possession can be many different things to different people. For some, it may be a loved one; for others it may be something of great value; and for still others, it represents the dreams that lie buried deep in our hearts—the dreams that give us hope for a better tomorrow.

In Genesis 42-43, Jacob is faced with just such a struggle. He has already lost his son, Joseph, and now he is being asked to release Benjamin, his youngest son, to the care of his brothers as they journey back to Egypt to get food during the great famine. For Jacob, this is a supreme sacrifice because Benjamin was the last of his children from the wife that he loved most. His choice was either to see all his family starve or allow Benjamin to be taken to Egypt, knowing he might never see him again.

We share in Jacob's dilemma as we prepare to release our children from the security of home into the world. Whether they are leaving home to begin college, get married, join the armed forces, or move away to the mission field, our heart cries out to keep them safe and close by us where they can be protected; but we know we must let them go. Or maybe our dilemma lies in placing a dream on hold while we attend to more pressing matters that life requires. We may arrive at the natural conclusion that our dream may never be fulfilled when in fact, it may simply be a matter of timing—God's perfect timing. Waiting is never easy, and this is especially true when we see others living their dreams while we wait patiently for ours to begin. Or perhaps it is a relationship that we had hoped would take on a different meaning only to see it fall to pieces. In all of these instances, we must learn the challenging task of letting go and trusting God.

We see in Jacob's struggle that initially he was so reluctant to release Benjamin to his brothers that he wouldn't let him go. He complained loudly to his sons, asking them why they had even mentioned that they had a brother. And even after he agreed to release Benjamin, he was so sad and depressed that he really believed that he might die from the pain if his son didn't return (Genesis 42:38). However, the famine was so intense that he had no choice but to let Benjamin go (Genesis 43:1). Until he settled this in his heart and requested God's mercy, he wasn't able to do what he needed to do. But even when he did do this, he counted the cost with great sadness and said, *"And if I must bear the anguish of their deaths then so be it"* (Genesis 43:13).

I have thought of this precious man's words over and over again. Have we counted the cost of releasing everything that we hold dear into God's hands? Can we truly say, "Lord, even if things don't turn out exactly as I would want, I can deal with it as long as You are there"?

Just as Jacob did, we are all faced with "famines" in our land. You may be suffering from an empty nest, or living in an unloving marriage that seems to be dead. You may have lost a job and wonder how you are going to pay the mortgage. Your dreams of happiness may seem so remote that you can't imagine how any good thing will ever happen to you again. And yet we know that God is able to do exceedingly, abundantly, more than we can ever ask or imagine (Ephesians 3:20). In fact, only He can remove the famine that may exist in your life today and give you renewed hope.

As I ponder all these things, I am comforted by one prevailing thought: It was when Jacob moved out in faith, trusting God with the outcome that he received all that God had for him. By sending Benjamin to Egypt, not only did Jacob ultimately see him again, but also the dream that he thought wasn't even possible became a reality—he also saw Joseph, the beloved son that he thought was dead! Just think what might have happened had he not released what he valued most.

Let us learn the lesson that Jacob's life teaches us. We do not have to be afraid when we place everything that we hold dear into

God's hand. His desire is always to bless us, and His plans for us are always good. His view of us is always from the perspective of eternity. When we release all we hold that is precious to Him, it leaves our hands open and ready to be filled by His very best.

Week 8 Memory Verse

Trust in the Lord with all your heart; do not depend on your own understanding. Seek his will in all you do, and he will show you which path to take (Proverbs 3:5-6).

Daily Quiet Reflections

Examine your values and priorities. What is most important to you?
_____
_____

After reviewing your list, in what areas have you not acknowledged God's sovereignty?
_____
_____

Are there some areas that, like Jacob, you are reluctant to release to God? If so, what are they?
_____
_____

Review this week's memory verse. How can you take action on this verse in your life today?
_____
_____

What does it mean to trust the Lord with all your heart?
_____
_____

Take time to pray and visualize yourself giving God your precious possessions for safekeeping.

⇥ Week 9: Enduring the Wait ⇤

I've been thinking often lately about the following passage of Scripture: *"But those that wait upon the Lord shall renew their strength. They shall mount up with wings like eagles. They shall run and not become weary. They shall walk and not faint"* (Isaiah 40:31).

There are different types of waiting. There is waiting like a bride right before the bridal procession song begins. There is waiting for your name to be called as one of the five finalists in a pageant. But there are other types of waiting such as the sad waiting to say a last goodbye at the funeral of a loved one. And the long waiting for the results of a medical report after an unusual spot has appeared on an x-ray.

All of these scenes from life describe waiting and immediately bring to mind all the emotion that goes with them. But God's Word describes what happens when a person waits on the Lord. He says our strength will be renewed. We will be able to fly like eagles, run without becoming weary, and walk without fainting.

How different waiting on the Lord should be. The focus should not be on the present circumstances that require us to wait; instead, the focus is on Him. When we focus on Him and His infinite love for us, the circumstances begin to pale in comparison.

But how do we stay focused on Him when circumstances overwhelm us? How do we continue to look to God when everything in us demands that we try to rectify, get out of, or deny completely the problem that is staring us in the face?

We do it by remembering the goodness of God. We remind ourselves of His promises to us in His Word. He said, *"I am with you always"* (Matthew 28:20). Since He has promised that He is with us always, then He is there in the middle of any circumstance we face. But most importantly, we know that He loves us; He proved this by giving His life for us. Won't He surely show Himself faithful to us when we trust in Him?

Let us not see our circumstances as too big for God. Remember that He is the Creator of the entire universe. The winds and the waves obey Him. The sun comes up each morning because He commands it to do so, and the evening stars appear in the sky in obedience to Him. Think about the majesty of that! You can be renewed while you wait on the Lord and find strength in knowing that even the hairs of your head are numbered (Matthew 10:30). You are known to God, and you are precious to Him.

So, if you find yourself waiting today, be secure while you wait; and know that He cares so much for you.

52 Weeks of WOW Faith

Week 9 Memory Verse

But those that wait upon the Lord shall renew their strength. They shall mount up with wings like eagles. They shall run and not become weary. They shall walk and not faint (Isaiah 40:31).

Daily Quiet Reflections

What have been some times when you found yourself waiting on the Lord?
_____
_____

What is your concept of God, especially as revealed through Jesus?
_____
_____

What about Jesus' nature assures you that there is value in waiting on God?
_____
_____

What has been the most difficult part of waiting for you?
_____
_____

This week's memory verse says that when we wait on the Lord, our strength will be renewed. What have been some ways that the Lord has renewed your strength?
_____
_____

How has this helped you when you found yourself waiting for God at other times?
_____
_____

→ Week 10: Running Your Race ←

Last weekend, I went out to do my normal five mile jog. I was running along at my regular pace, which is about an eleven minute mile. Compared to my average in college (six minutes), this is tremendously slow; but I have been out of college for over twenty years and am simply glad to be still running As I was finishing my fourth mile and beginning mile five, I decided to push myself and try to finish the last mile in ten minutes. I immediately picked up the pace, but it was such a struggle since I was already tired from having run the previous four miles.

So there I was running with my tongue hanging out when another jogger glided by me as though he were on roller blades. In fact, I looked down at his jogging shoes to see if he had wheels on them, which would explain his fast pace—but of course he didn't. So I thought to myself, *Try to keep up with him.* And the race began! The only problem was that he was winning!

Realizing that I was surely going to come in second, I thought, *Just try and keep him in sight.* So I ran along doggedly behind him just trying to keep him in view before the sun set. Past trees, and squirrels, and around curves and down molehills I ran. He seemed to get further away and increased the distance between us. I thought, *I had better finish this before it's so dark I can't see the path he is taking.*

It was then that I heard God's still, small voice deep inside me. He seemed to be saying that in order to follow Him in life, we must always keep Him in our sights and run our own race. When we take our eyes off Him and start looking at other joggers, we can easily go down a wrong path or take a wrong turn and get lost by making decisions that are not His best plan for us. My head was spinning as I grappled with the truth of this message. (My head was also spinning because I was trying to keep that jogger in sight.)

I realized later as I finished that last mile (in ten minutes, I might add) that we must each run our own race, always keeping our focus on God no matter what may be happening to us at any given moment. It is easy to become distracted and head down a distant path that leads to nowhere. So often we get caught up with what others are doing and wonder whether we are keeping up with them. We become distracted by the news and world events and wonder if we should follow the path that everyone else seems to be taking. We have no way of knowing whether the path they are on is the one that is right for us, or if the pace they are keeping is a pace that we need to keep.

But when our focus is on God, we have the assurance of knowing that He always chooses the right path for us. When He picks up the pace, He gives us the strength to persevere. We can rest in the fact He already has the end in sight, and it is glorious! We have only to keep our legs moving and enjoy the scenery. When we run our own race—the one that God has destined for us since the beginning of time—we find that He always takes us safely across the finish line.

Week 10 Memory Verse

So let us lay aside every weight, and the sin which so easily ensnares us, and let us run with endurance the race that is set before us, looking unto Jesus, the author and finisher of our faith, who for the joy that was set before Him endured the cross, despising the shame, and has sat down at the right hand of the throne of God. (Hebrews 12:1-2 HCSB).

Daily Quiet Reflections

What have been some key causes to taking your eyes off Jesus while running your race of faith?
_____
_____

While Jesus was conducting His ministry on earth, what were some essential habits that He practiced to stay focused on His goals?
_____
_____

When facing discouragement, losing sight of the big picture is not difficult. What are some ways that you can remain focused when faced with the temptation to accept defeat?
_____
_____

Sometimes, distractions that hinder our progress in life can be difficult to eliminate. The memory verse encourages us to "lay aside every weight, and the sin which so easily ensnares us." What are some sins in your life that you need to lay aside?
_____
_____

In what ways do you think your faith in Jesus can assist you in ending sinful habits that hamper your relationship with Him?
_____
_____

Pray and ask God to reveal to you those sins that grieve His heart and give you the strength to eliminate those from your life.

Week 11: In the Fire With God

Faith is not simply a matter of believing that God will do what we think is best for us. Faith is believing that whatever God does is best, regardless of how it seems to affect us. This concept is difficult to put into practice! I recently finished a study of Daniel, and I was once again drawn in by the heroes of our faith. When I think of the three Hebrew boys and their response to King Nebuchadnezzar when he demanded that they bow down and worship the golden image, I am amazed. Very confidently, they declared they would not bow down no matter what the consequences. Instead, they were prepared to die for their convictions. They were certain of one thing: no matter what God chose to do in those circumstances, it would be the best outcome for them—even if it were death. (Read this biblical account in Daniel 3.)

How many of us truly can say we have faith like that? Typically, we have figured out a few scenarios that we believe to be best for us. We would certainly never choose to get thrown into a fire! In fact, most of us would run in the opposite direction from any scenario that included being burned alive. But there are some things worth dying for, and we must know with certainty what those are. When we say that we are believers in Christ, would we be willing to die for that belief? If we were threatened with death unless we renounced Christ, would we remain loyal until the end?

That is what the Hebrew boys were willing to risk. They were convinced that their lives were meaningless if they were not loyal to their God. Did you notice that even after they were thrown into the fire and were observed walking freely about with what appeared to be the Son of God, they made no attempt to get out of the fire? Think about this: They are in the fire, they're not on fire, the ropes that had bound them have burned off, and they are walking around with God. Wouldn't you think they would have taken this opportunity to get out of that fire? Instead, Scriptures record that King Nebuchadnezzar came to the mouth of the furnace and shouted,

"Shadrach, Meshach, and Abednego, servants of the Most High God, come out! Come here!' So Shadrach, Meshach, and Abednego stepped out of the fire (Daniel 3:26).

It wasn't until the king demanded that they come out of the fire that they did. I think the Hebrew boys already knew something that many of us have still to learn: Being anywhere with God is better than being any other place without Him. Even when we find ourselves in the middle of a firestorm, it is the best place to be if God is there too. Believers should "not think it strange concerning the fiery trial" that we face (1 Peter 4:12) because it is often during these times that our faith is strengthened. Our trials provide us with an opportunity to trust God.

Let us strive to follow the example so powerfully demonstrated in the story of Shadrach, Meshach, and Abednego. Resolve in your heart that no matter what the future holds, you will hold onto God. If God is in the middle of your fiery circumstances, you can rest assured that you are safe; and your future is certain because you are trusting in Him.

Week 11 Memory Verse

Friends, when life gets really difficult, don't jump to the conclusion that God isn't on the job. Instead, be glad that you are in the very thick of what Christ experienced. This is a spiritual refining process, with glory just around the corner (1 Peter 4:12-13 MSG).

Daily Quiet Reflections

Review this week's memory verse. When going through a difficult season, what does God promise will be the outcome in your life?

_____
_____

What do you think is the purpose of a spiritual refining process?

_____
_____

What are some of the lessons that you can take away from the story in Daniel 3?

_____
_____

One way that we can endure difficult times is to focus on how big God is versus how big our circumstances are. In what ways is God bigger than your current circumstances?

_____
_____

Read 1 Peter 5:6-7. Based on this Scripture, what are we promised that God will do when we humble ourselves?

_____
_____

Identify your present lists of concerns. Take this list to God during your prayer time and review the list with Him. Finally, visualize yourself giving your list to Him and leaving it there.

_____
_____

⇢ Week 12: Developing a Habit of Thanks ⇠

"And the Lord said, 'My people are long on askin' and short on thankin'." A dear woman of God spoke those words recently at a study I was attending. For some reason, this statement resonated with me as I was reminded of all the times I have rushed past my thanks to God on my way to asking Him for something else. "Thank you, God, for letting those medical tests come back negative. Now God, could you please give me . . ." On and on the list of requests go. In reflecting on this, I wondered how God must feel when His children can barely get out a word of thanks before going on to the next petition. God beautifully demonstrated this one day through my own child.

Elise came bounding down the stairs a few weeks ago with a typed list of what she wanted to be sure I included in her Easter basket this year. (Yes, even as a teen, she still wants a basket for Easter!) Her father and I had recently spent a significant amount of money on a pageant she had been involved in, and I believed that her Easter basket had already "runneth over." Wrong! As I reviewed her list, I shook my head thinking, *I can't believe this child has the nerve to ask for a deluxe Easter basket after the money we just spent on her!* Of course, she had been very grateful, but her gratitude had lasted for about a nano-second before she was thinking about something else that she wanted. And that's when it hit me—that is exactly the way I am with God sometimes! The truth is, and I'm ashamed to admit it, I have a tendency to be "long on askin' and short on thankin'"! Have you found that to be true in your own life?

If so, choose to be different today. Stop and make a list of all the things you have to be grateful for and see it as God's daily Easter basket made especially for you, His dear child. God wants to bless His children. We don't constantly have to ask Him for what we need because He already knows, and He loves to give good gifts to us. It is when we give thanks that our hope is restored because we are reminded of all He has done for us in the past.

I made a decision recently to take a break from asking God for things and instead began to focus on being thankful. The most amazing result has taken place! He continues to give! I simply can't outrun His blessings because they are new every day. I learned something else about God from my dear daughter, and that is that even though she can be a little self-absorbed at times, that doesn't change the way I feel about her. I'm truly nuts about her! As a result, it occurred to me that even when I am totally self-absorbed, God's love for me doesn't change either. He is still nuts about me too! And the same is true of you!

Let tomorrow be the start of a new day, a day of thanksgiving where we truly thank Him for His sovereignty, the life He has given us, and all His many, many, blessings. Let's develop a habit of thanks.

Week 12 Memory Verse

In everything give thanks; for this is the will of God in Christ Jesus for you (Thessalonians 5:18 NKJV).

Daily Quiet Reflections

Make a list of everything for which you can give thanks. Add at least one new thing each day for a week. Use this list to thank God for blessings in your life.

Our thankfulness to God should not change based on our circumstances. How does the memory verse this week reveal that truth?

Read Proverbs 3:5-6 (week seven's memory verse). Why is it important for us not to "lean on our understanding"?

Think about some events or circumstances in your past for which you were not initially thankful. How has the passage of time helped you to realize the truth stated in Romans 8:28?

Of all of God's blessings in your life, which are you most thankful for and why?

End your quiet time today once again thanking God for who He is and what He is doing in your life.

➤ Week 13: Waiting on God's Timing ❈

Have you ever been anxious to get started on something you believe God has asked you to do, maybe a new area of ministry or a new season of your life, only to have everything grind to a halt with no explanation?

Something like that happened to Balaam, a man that lived during the time of Moses. Balaam had been asked by King Balak to join him against the people of Israel because King Balak feared the Israelites. When Balaam consulted God about this, he was told not to do it because the people of Israel were blessed. However, later God released Balaam to join King Balak, while stating clearly that Balaam was only to speak those words to King Balak that were specifically given to him by God.

Something peculiar happened when Balaam set out on his journey. His donkey began acting strangely while he was on the road and at one point refused to move forward! This was odd behavior because his donkey was normally quite obedient. Despite the beatings he received from Balaam, that donkey would not move! In fact, the donkey was miraculously able to talk and asked Balaam, "Why do you keep beating me?" The donkey could see what Balaam could not see—an angel blocking his path. Finally, when it became clear that Balaam was not getting the message, the Lord opened Balaam's eyes so that he could see the angel and understand that it was God that was blocking his path.

Spiritual truths from this story that apply to our lives beg to be explored. First, God initially forbade Balaam to do what Balak had asked him to do. Second, when Balak persisted in his request to have Balaam join him, God gave Balaam permission to go but told him to do only what He told him to do. Third, Balaam obeyed God and went with Balak's men. But then it says, "God was furious with Balaam that he was going and He sent an angel to block his way" (Numbers 22:22). Why would God give these orders but later change them? We experience similar occurrences in life when God gives us specific instructions on a matter but tells us to stick close to Him daily so that we are prepared to change at a moment's notice if need be.

Sometimes God will tell us to do something, while instructing us to wait on Him to do it. In our eagerness to do God's will, we set out on our own and begin doing it in our own strength and in our own way. We begin to experience road blocks in areas that would normally be a piece of cake. But instead of us stopping to reassess if we are still on point or if we have proceeded ahead of God, we move blindly ahead on our path, stubbornly resisting everything that points us back to God just as Balaam did.

The good news is that God will not allow us to do that. We can be confident that He will grab our attention because He has promised that even if we stumble, He will not allow us to fall (Psalm 37:24). The story of Balaam ends where he proclaims blessings on Israel—not by his normal means of understanding God's message, but by the Spirit of God coming upon him to speak prophetically through him.

We see one man's spiritual journey from novice to giant. As he grows and develops in his relationship with God, he becomes more sensitized to His presence and more able to hear His voice. In the same way, we must also develop in our own spiritual journey, learning to continue to do what God has already instructed us to do. We must do this in His timing and in His way. God wants us to be zealous about doing His will but also to be zealous about His timing. We know that any good work that God has started in our lives, He will complete!

Week 13 Memory Verse

Your own ears will hear him. Right behind you a voice will say, "This is the way you should go" (Isaiah 30:21).

Daily Quiet Reflections

Read this week's memory verse again. What is the promise that we receive from this passage of Scripture?
___
___

Identify a time when you were certain of God's direction on what to do but experienced a barrier that hampered your progress. How did you handle this?
___
___

What would you do differently based on the story of Balaam?
___
___

Why is waiting on God's timing important in accomplishing His purposes?
___
___

How do you balance the tendency to run ahead of God versus lagging behind Him?
___
___

What is the most important action you can take today to stay within God's timing?
___
___

⇥ Week 14: God's Passion ⇤

Have you ever wondered what God's passion is? I did and searched the Scriptures for the answer. I stumbled upon an amazing passage: *"He is a God who is passionate about his relationship with you"* (Exodus 34:14). What an amazing thought! The God of the universe is passionate about His relationship with us. In meditating on this wonderful revelation, I begin to think about those people in my life for whom I feel passion. This is a thought-provoking word, one we normally equate with feelings for a lover, a beloved child, or a dear parent. What about areas of our life that provoke passion? Many of us have a very strong passion for a big bowl of ice cream or a new pair of shoes.

Actually, the intent in this passage seems to describe the importance of God's feelings about His relationship with us as well as His feelings about you and me. For example, I am passionate about my relationship with my husband and daughter. I wouldn't want my husband to look with passion at any other woman, and I wouldn't want my daughter to call anyone else "Mom" but me. They belong to me, and therefore their relationship with me is unique. I am my husband's only wife and my daughter's only mother. There is no one else who should hold those places in their lives or in their hearts because it is my place and only mine. Of course, each of them has a unique place in my heart and in my life as well.

I believe this is the idea that God conveys in the Exodus passage. Our relationship with Him is special, unique, and cherished. He is passionate about His relationship with you and me because He wants it to be unique, special, and cherished by us as well. Is it? We must each determine whether we share God's passion. When we make this passion the focus of our lives, then we can truly experience a supernatural, all-encompassing intimacy with Him that only He can provide. In this we will find true rest for our souls.

The next time you wonder, *What is God's passion?*, remember that His passion is YOU!

Week 14 Memory Verse

For God loved the world so much that he gave his one and only Son, so that everyone who believes in him will not perish but have eternal life (John 3:16).

Daily Quiet Reflections

How does knowing that God is passionate about you impact you today?
_____
_____

Many times we don't always *feel* as though God loves us. What are some ways that God has demonstrated His love towards you?
_____
_____

What are some ways that you can demonstrate that you love God?
_____
_____

Review this week's memory verse. How has the gift of God's Son, Jesus, impacted your life?
_____
_____

How does this gift demonstrate God's supreme passion for you?
_____
_____

What is your response to God's gift?
_____
_____

✧ Week 15: Walking in Your Gethsemane ✧

(Read: Matthew 26:39, Mark 14:36, Luke 22:41)

Have you ever been reluctant to accept what you believed was God's plan for your life? Have you ever had your own personal Gethsemane—a time that you struggled with the direction you believed God was taking you on in your life's journey?

When we read the story of Jesus in the garden of Gethsemane, we remember that His prayer ended with, "Not my will but Yours be done." But what about the beginning? When Jesus first began petitioning His heavenly Father, His initial request was, "Father, is there any other way for this to be done?"

I love the humanness of that question. It reveals how Jesus truly was One who experienced all the different emotions that we do—yet He never sinned. Clearly, at this point He was very troubled by the path He was about to take. He deeply felt the weight of our sins, and He knew that it was necessary to offer a living sacrifice to God on our behalf. And yet in the midst of all this, He still wanted to confirm with His Father once again that this plan was perfect.

So often our journeys will take us on paths that are not easy. We may be troubled by our circumstances and even tempted to think that God doesn't have a good plan for our lives. Or we may be tempted to believe the plan He has for us isn't the best. We may even be proud enough to believe that we have a better plan for our lives and may struggle to offer God some assistance.

When you are tempted to say, "Father, isn't there another way that this can be done?" remember how Jesus finished His prayer, "not My will, Father, but Yours be done." How was He able to say that in the middle of His circumstances? Because He chose to believe God despite His circumstances. He placed all His hope in God. Decide today to believe that God's plan is best, and He is greater than any circumstances you face. When in your Gethsemane, trust God!

Week 15 Memory Verse

"For I know the plans I have for you," says the Lord. "They are plans for good and not for disaster, to give you a future and a hope" (Jeremiah 29:11).

Daily Quiet Reflections

What are some of the plans that you have for your future?
_____
_____

How can you be sure that these are plans that are God-given versus self-imposed?
_____
_____

How have you handled those times when your plans haven't worked out the way you wanted?
_____
_____

What can be learned from Jesus' example in Gethsemane?
_____
_____

How does this week's memory verse help you in dealing with plans that didn't succeed or meet your expectations?
_____
_____

Pray and ask God to help you to trust in His plans for your life and His ability to accomplish what will bless you and glorify Him.

❧ Week 16: The Gift of Pain ☙

All of us wish that we could lead a life free from pain and suffering; and yet if we were granted that wish, what would we lose in the process? We know that physical pain has its benefits. If I place my hand on a hot iron, the sensation of pain is what lets me know that my hand is in danger of being burned. Without the pain caused by my action, my body would be defenseless in situations that could be life threatening.

The same can be said of our spiritual and emotional pain. When our consciences are disturbed or in pain, it can be warning us of some moral danger or some evil that could destroy us emotionally or spiritually. When we are afraid, it sensitizes us to situations that require us to fight or flee. Therefore, pain is a natural part of our human experience, and it is that which often draws out aspects of God's character that we would fail to know or experience had pain not been the impetus.

What are some of the characteristics of God that pain reveals? The pain of loss brings on God's immeasurable comfort. The pain of suffering a physical ailment causes us to experience His unfathomable strength. The pain of loneliness often causes us to know the great depth of His love and friendship. Imagine all that would be missed in knowing Him were it not for our times of pain and suffering. Could it be that pain truly is the gift that no one wants but that everyone needs?

God revealed one of the purposes for pain best through the life of the apostle Paul when on three separate occasions Paul pleaded with God to remove his pain. God's response was, "My grace is sufficient for you, for my strength is made perfect in weakness" (2 Corinthians 12:9 NKJV).

In our pain and in our suffering, God's strength is perfected in us; and we come to know how totally dependent we are upon Him. But more importantly, we come to know the meaning of His Hebrew name, *El Shaddai*, which means, "all-sufficient One." He is everything we need to withstand the difficulties that accompany our pain, and He is compassionate towards us during our suffering. None of us can avoid what is inevitably a part of life, but our view of pain can change as we move closer into God's embrace.

Week 16 Memory Verse

My grace is sufficient for you, for my strength is made perfect in weakness (2 Corinthians 12:9 NKJV).

Daily Quiet Reflections

Read this week's memory verse. How do you believe God's strength is made perfect in our weakness?
___
___

What have been the most powerful lessons you have learned during a time of pain or suffering?
___
___

Read Job 1:20-22. The story of Job is one of extreme suffering. After Job had lost everything that was important to him, what was his response?
___
___

What was unique about Job's relationship with God that gave him the ability to respond in this manner?
___
___

What are some ways that you can have that same type of relationship with God?
___
___

If you are going through a time of suffering, pray today that God will make this week's memory verse a reality in your life.

✧ Week 17: Confidence During the Storm ✦

When the fourth most intense Atlantic hurricane ever recorded, Hurricane Rita, threatened the Galveston/Houston area, I began to reflect on all I knew about weathering the storm. Having lived on the Gulf Coast all my life, I have prepared for many storms before, but this was different. The level of panic in the community was heightened by the tragic events in New Orleans, and I'm sure that it will be known in the future as the "Katrina factor." As we all set about preparing for what promised to be the worst storm in our history, I thought, *Father God, what do You have to say about all this?*

As He so often does, His gentle voice reminded me to pray. And so I did. In weathering any storm, it is important to remember one truth: God never changes. This gives us confidence no matter what the circumstances. We evacuated not knowing whether we would have a home to return to, and yet we had confidence that God was Lord over our circumstances and that He is sovereign. Our lives are in His hands, and I can't think of a better place to be. And so we journeyed on for many hours not knowing what the outcome would be, but knowing that our God is faithful to His children. We trusted that He would take care of us, and He did.

Today I must agree with the psalmist who said,

Oh, give thanks to the Lord, for He is good!
For His mercy endures forever.

Oh, give thanks to the God of gods!
For His mercy endures forever.

Oh, give thanks to the Lord of lords!
For His mercy endures forever.

To Him who alone does great wonders,
For His mercy endures forever;

To Him who by wisdom made the heavens,
For His mercy endures forever;

To Him who laid out the earth above the waters,
For His mercy endures forever;

To Him who made great lights,
For His mercy endures forever—

The sun to rule by day,
For His mercy endures forever;

The moon and stars to rule by night,
For His mercy endures forever;

Who remembered us in our lowly state,
For His mercy endures forever;

And rescued us from our enemies,
For His mercy endures forever;

Who gives food to all flesh,
For His mercy endures forever.

(Who dissipated Hurricane Rita and limited her destruction,
For His mercy endures forever.) *

Oh, give thanks to the God of heaven!
For His mercy endures forever
(Psalm 136:1-9, 23-26 NKJV, *extra verse added for emphasis).

No matter what storm of life you face today, remember that our God is bigger than any storm, and His mercy endures forever!

Week 17 Memory Verse

Give thanks to the Lord, for he is good! His faithful love endures forever (Psalm 136:1 NKJV).

Daily Quiet Reflections

What are some of the current storms that you are enduring in life today?
_____
_____

What is your response to these storms?
_____
_____

What are some of the reasons God allows us to have stormy times in life?
_____
_____

How has your faith in God grown as a result of past storms?
_____
_____

What are some lessons learned from your life's storms?
_____
_____

Read Luke 8:22-25. What are some principles from this story that you can apply to your life?
_____
_____

✦ Week 18: The Temptation To Compromise ✦

My dear former pastor, John Osteen, used to say many times, "You have to fight life through." He meant that life is not always going to be easy, and there will always be something that keeps you on your knees. You have to be more determined to follow hard after God so you won't get beaten down by your circumstances. Pastor Osteen was saying to refuse compromise, stand strong, and keep fighting until you have all that God has for you!

This was great advice that I have often thought of while going through my own life's struggles. We all face situations that have tempted us to concede instead of continue to fight. It may be a temptation to compromise our principles, values, or beliefs. We don't wake up thinking, *Today, I'm going to compromise.* Instead, it gradually happens through small decisions made day by day, and before long, we are looking up from a pit only to realize that we haven't been standing firm. We've been sliding down the slippery slope of compromise.

This begins when we lose sight of the big picture for our lives. We get busy going through our ritual of living, and then a difficult circumstance comes along—a trial or a test of our faith. In a weakened state, finding a shortcut out of a trial may be an easy solution; but in doing so, we lose the greater opportunity and may fall short of receiving the better plan that God has for us.

Think about the time that Jesus was tempted during His forty days in the wilderness. The word *wilderness* conjures up pictures of loneliness, depravity, and isolation. Jesus was weak from lack of food, and the enemy already knew who Jesus was and felt threatened by Him. But more importantly, he felt threatened by the impact that Jesus' life would have on humanity. He had to have a plan—one that would cause Jesus to compromise. If he could accomplish that, he knew that the greater plan that God had for Jesus' life would be destroyed. And so he set about offering Jesus an opportunity to compromise. He waited until Jesus was at His lowest point and suggested a shortcut for having authority over the earth. "Just imagine," he whispered, "all this could be Yours if You will only worship before me." If Jesus had not been filled with the Holy Spirit, He could have thought to himself, *I could have all this and completely avoid the cross. It wouldn't be too difficult to do. I could be the ruler over the earth and have authority to save mankind too.*

But as we know, Jesus didn't think this way because He knew it wasn't true. He knew God's plan was more difficult, but He also knew it was better. So instead of compromising, He chose to fight life through all the way to the cross. In the end, He not only accomplished God's plan for humanity, but He also was elevated to a place of authority at the right hand of God. Where would we be if He had taken the easy way out and not made the decision to fight life through? Thank God, Jesus remembered the big picture for His life and wanted that more than anything the enemy could offer Him.

What about you? Are you compromising or standing firm? Do you realize, "Greater is he that is in you, than he that is in the world" (1 John 4:4 KJV)? The same source of power that Jesus had exists for you today. God has a big plan for your life. The enemy is threatened by that plan and knows the impact you will have on your generation. Don't compromise and take the easy route. Instead, stand firm, be strong, and remember to fight life through!

Week 18 Memory Verse

But you belong to God, my dear children. You have already won a victory over those people, because the Spirit who lives in you is greater than the spirit who lives in the world (1 John 4:4).

Daily Quiet Reflections

Read this week's memory verse again. How will knowing that the Spirit of God in you is greater than the one in the world help you in your present circumstances?

Think of a time when you compromised your beliefs. What were the reasons that you compromised?

What were the consequences of compromising?

What should you do the next time you are tempted to compromise?

What impact do you believe God wants you to have on your generation?

Spend time in prayer asking God to give you the courage to resist the temptation to compromise.

⇾ Week 19: Standing Firm Against Fear ⇽

While on a business trip to San Antonio, Texas, I found myself with some free time and decided to visit the Alamo. For Texans, the Alamo is a symbol of the fight for freedom. It serves as a reminder to be brave and not let fear of an enemy stop the pursuit of freedom at any cost. At this location, a small band of brave men fought against terrible odds and many gave their lives in order to live independently of Mexico. In fact, Juan Seguin, a colonel in the Texas army and one of only a handful of survivors, said the men of the Alamo preferred to die rather than live in fear and under a rule of tyranny. And die they did.

I pondered what would give these men the courage to leave their families for something that they knew would result in never seeing them again. I believe part of it must have been that they had simply had enough. They were tired of living in fear, and that was what motivated them to desire something better for their loved ones. Their willingness to give their lives left a legacy that said, "I refuse to live in fear any more."

This caused me to reflect on what it would take for many of us to come to a point where we have had enough. By this, I mean the tyranny that is often caused by the enemy of our souls. Aren't we also guilty of allowing him to intimidate us and cause us to be afraid? We so often go through our lives being pushed around by a tyrant, never stopping to think about what is causing our fear.

The reasons for our fear could be anything. You name it, and we've probably been afraid of it at some point or another. It could be the fear of losing our health, the fear of something happening to our kids, the fear of the future, the fear of losing our jobs, and the big one . . . the fear of living an insignificant life. The list is endless. It occurred to me after my visit to the Alamo that I for one have had enough! The Word of God says that He does not give us a spirit of fear but of confidence and of a sound mind (2 Timothy 1:7). As such, we—like the men at the Alamo—must refuse to live another day of our lives being afraid. We must believe what God says about us, bravely face our tomorrows without fear, and no longer accept intimidation. We may not know what the future holds, but we do know who holds the future and can be confident that He will carry us safely through our circumstances.

When you are tempted to be afraid, remind yourself of what we in Texas are known to say, "Remember the Alamo!" Because our days of fear are finished. Thank God!

Week 19 Memory Verse

For God has not given us a spirit of fear and timidity, but of power, love, and self-discipline (2 Timothy 1:7).

Daily Quiet Reflections

Read the memory verse for this week again. Based on this passage of Scripture, what do you think God wants you to be that you have not been?
_____
_____

What are some of these fears that exist in your life today?
_____
_____

What does a spirit of power produce in your life that a spirit of fear hinders?
_____
_____

How can you best apply the truth of the memory verse to your life today?
_____
_____

Since God has already given us a spirit of power, love, and self-confidence, what do you believe is the best way for you to access these gifts?
_____
_____

Pray that the spirit of power, love, and self-discipline will become evident in your life today.

⇾ Week 20: God's Dream for Us ⇽

Have you ever had a big dream—a dream of doing something that you knew you were born to do? What's keeping you from fulfilling your dream?

I believe we were all born with a deep-seated desire to do something special with our lives—something that only we can do. This dream was placed in our hearts when we were born, but so often we get busy with living and over time forget the dream. Before we know it, the dream is but a distant memory.

But there is good news! It's not too late to start living the dream. In fact, that subtle, tender longing you feel deep in your heart is the dream pressing its way back into your consciousness saying, *Why did you let me go?* It is a question worth asking ourselves. If God has placed a dream in your heart, isn't it worth the effort to actually live it?

Of course, it's not easy pursuing a dream. In fact, there may be times that it seems impossible. Oh, but the journey is more than worth it. As we pursue the dreams of our lives, we have a glimpse of heaven. For you see, God had a dream too. His dream was to have all His children return to live with Him in heaven for eternity. And so He set a plan in motion, the plan of salvation. God came down from heaven in the form of a man—the man we know as Jesus, the Messiah—fully man, yet fully God. He came so that through Him we would know the way home. He said that if anyone would believe in Him and follow Him, He would take them back to spend eternity with Him (John 3:16).

God's dream wasn't easy to fulfill. He came, He lived, and He was crucified as a sacrifice for us. Taking our sins upon Himself, He paid the price for our full ticket home. What an amazing gift! What an amazing dream! But it is no longer just a dream. It actually happened. And now through Jesus' resurrection, each of us can be called the daughters and sons of God by accepting His free gift of salvation.

God didn't merely have a dream; He did something about it. Won't you do the same? If you have never accepted Jesus as your Lord and Savior, this gift is for you. Pray for Him to come into your heart and begin living the dream today.

Week 20 Memory Verse

And I am sure that God, who began the good work within you, will continue his work until it is finally finished on that day when Christ Jesus comes back again (Philippians 1:6).

Daily Quiet Reflections

What is the one thing you would like to accomplish before the end of your life?
_____
_____

How will accomplishing this bless God? Bless others?
_____
_____

What is keeping you from fulfilling this dream?
_____
_____

What steps could you take today that would move you closer to achieving all of which you are capable?
_____
_____

Read this week's memory verse. What is "the good work" that you believe God has started in you?
_____
_____

What does God promise through the passage of Scripture?
_____
_____

➔ Week 21: Help for Life's Giants ✦

Long ago, when I was in elementary school, there was a little boy who was the resident bully. All the kids were afraid of him because he was always threatening to beat up somebody. Somehow, I found myself on the receiving end of his threats, and I was scared! Every day he would torment me and tell me how he was going to beat me up after school. He became the "Goliath" in my life. This boy was a giant so big that he invaded all my thoughts. This went on for what seemed like forever, and I begin to feel ill before school and begged my mother not to make me go.

Eventually, my mother discerned what the root cause of my illness was and unbeknownst to me, she decided to stake out my pathway home from school so that she could catch the bully in action. On that particular day, I was walking home and the bully was right behind me, shoving me and warning me of further danger. I was trying not to cry and wondered if this would be the day that he acted on his threats. All of a sudden, from out of nowhere, my mom popped up from behind a parked car where she had been hiding in wait for me and the bully. I was never so happy to see her in my life! I immediately ran to her and hid behind her skirts as she dealt with the bully. I felt such courage flow through me as my mother admonished him to stop his bad behavior and encouraged him to be kind to those smaller than he was. From that day forward, I never had any more problems with that bully. In fact, he became one of my protectors!

How often have we had giant bullies that invaded our lives? Maybe it's the giant of worry or the giant of circumstances. They invade our thoughts as we try to figure out how on earth we will overcome a particular problem. Day after day, we struggle in our own minds and often become overwhelmed by the bully that is relentless and giant-like as we try to fight back in our own strength. And then, as though out of nowhere, we discover the presence of God and His desire to help us deal with those giants. Was He there all along? Is it possible that we focused so much on our giants that we forgot to cry out for help?

It reminded me of what the psalmist said during those times when he needed help to conquer the giants in his life:

I look up to the mountains—does my help come from there? My help comes from the Lord, who made the heavens and the earth! He will not let you stumble and fall; The one who watches over you will not sleep. Indeed, he who watches over Israel never tires and never sleeps. The Lord himself watches over you! The Lord stands beside you as your protective shade. The sun will not hurt you by day, nor the moon at night. The Lord keeps you from all evil and preserves your life (Psalm 121:1-7).

We should never forget that we have the ability to call on God when a giant enters our lives. Whether it is sickness, depression, heartache, loneliness, or anything that may come to overwhelm us, these challenges provide the perfect time for us to call on our heavenly Father for help. There are no giants too big or problems too small to enlist His help. He loves us, and He takes great pleasure in giving us the strength to continue. Just as my mother interceded on my behalf when I was being bullied at school, God is a diligent and protective parent that will hear and respond to our cries for help. He will not allow us to be destroyed.

So Goliaths, beware! Our God is a very present help in times of trouble!

Week 21 Memory Verse

The Lord will keep you from every kind of harm. He will watch over your life (Psalm 1:7).

Daily Quiet Reflections

Can you remember a time when you were especially fearful about your circumstances? How did you handle it?
___
___

What bullies in your life are dealing with today?
___
___

Read Psalm 121. What does God promise to do for you when you call on Him?
___
___

What is one thing you can do to remain in faith even if there are Goliath type circumstances that you face?
___
___

What may be some possible lessons that you can learn from your present situation?
___
___

Write a prayer to God thanking Him for his help with your Goliath.
___
___

✢ Week 22: God's Busy Schedule ✢

I endured a really nasty head cold recently, and as many of my friends know, I milked it for all it was worth. I had a good excuse to avoid doing anything I didn't feel like doing. At the top of that list was exercising. After all, I couldn't exercise because I was sick.

So I decided I needed a sick day. However, during my illness, I was rather busy watching God. I don't mean that I could actually see Him, but I certainly had a strong sense of Him. While watching, I discovered something very interesting: God keeps a really busy schedule!

Despite the affliction that caused me to curtail my activities, He never once took a break. I sensed Him when I woke up that morning and saw the sun attempting to rise on a very cloudy day. I sensed Him in the evening when I laid my head down on my pillow and thought how soft and comfortable it felt under my very stuffed-up head. I caught a glimpse of Him when my daughter brought me soup during her lunch break from school while I rested in my PJs in the middle of the afternoon. And I saw Him again when later my husband laid his hand on my forehead with concern because he thought I felt a little warm.

God was there when I sank down into a hot, soothing bubble bath that relieved my tired, aching muscles. And He was there when my best gal pal teasingly asked me how much longer I planned to whine about being sick. The warmth and ease of our longtime friendship made it easy for her to poke fun, and I could tell that God had visited me through our shared laughter.

Before this experience, I never gave a thought to how truly busy God is. He does so many great and awesome things that I had lost sight of the small, seemingly insignificant details that He takes care of each day. I'm so glad He's not only concerned about the big picture but makes Himself known in very ordinary ways. And suddenly, they become as extraordinary as He is.

And to think, I was able to discover His very busy schedule all because I decided to take a sick day.

Week 22 Memory Verse

For the Lord takes pleasure in His people; He will beautify the humble with salvation and adorn the wretched with victory (Psalm 149:4 AMP).

Daily Quiet Reflections

Try to recall an ordinary day when you sensed God's presence. What was He doing that made you know that He is even in the small details of life?
_____
_____

Read this week's memory verse again. How do you think the Lord takes pleasure in you?
_____
_____

What are some things about an ordinary day that bring you joy?
_____
_____

How can you learn to see God in the "everyday-ness" of life?
_____
_____

If Jesus appeared before you in person, in a tangible, visible form, what would you do?
_____
_____

What would you talk about with Him?
_____
_____

⇾ Week 23: Are You Speaking Blessings? ⇽

When our daughter was very small, my husband and I made a decision very early on to speak only blessings over her life and to give edifying descriptions of each season of her life. Consequently, we never viewed or described her season at the age of two as the "terrible two's." Instead, we called that time the "terrific two's." We went on to have the "tremendous three's," the "fantastic four's," the "fabulous five's," and so on. Even as a teenager, we have viewed this entire season of her life as the "thrilling teens"!

Not realizing it at the time, we soon discovered the spiritual value of our words and the power to influence her life experience. In a way, those words have proved to be direct from our mouths to God's ears as our daughter continues to grow in grace each day.

This point was really brought home to me as I read the amazing account of the Israelites as they sent a group of their leaders to spy out the Promised Land under the leadership of Moses. After returning, they were thrilled to report that the land was all God had said it would be; however, they were overwhelmed by the size of the people and the fortified cities. They declared there was no way they could take the land because they believed the land would devour them (Numbers 13:32-33). As a result, God said, *"I will do to you the very things you say"* (Numbers 14:28 NIV). And as we all know, none of that generation ever made it into the Promised Land. All of those that declared those words died without ever seeing it.

Think about it. God was listening to every word they said—both good and bad. Once they decided in their own minds that they would not be successful in obtaining the land God promised them, they spoke it into existence. From their mouths to God's ears, their words were manifested in their lives.

But what about the two spies who tried to reason with them and said, "We can take the land! God is with us and He will cause our success!"? Those two spies, Caleb and Joshua, were the only two from that generation that ever set foot in Canaan. Their words also reached God's ears. As they spoke confidence and acted in obedience to Him, He brought in the blessing of victory just as they declared.

What words are you speaking over your life? Are they words of blessing and edification? Are you expecting God's blessings in your life as you obey Him? Or do you get caught up in a cycle of negative words and self-condemnation?

Let us declare what is good, right, and holy into our lives. Our words have power. We should think about what we are speaking into our lives each day. The Scriptures say, *"The power of life and death are in the tongue"* (Proverbs 18:21). As our thoughts spill over into our words and ultimately into our actions, we impact today and our futures.

I want the words that God hears me speak to be ones He is delighted to hear, prompting Him to send more blessings my way. What about you?

Week 23 Memory Verse

Death and life are in the power of the tongue, and they who indulge in it shall eat the fruit of it (Proverbs 18:21 AMP).

Daily Quiet Reflections

What words are you speaking over your life?
___
___

Are they words of blessing and edification? Give examples of blessing you can speak now.
___
___

Are you expecting God's blessings in your life as you obey Him? If not, why not?
___
___

Do you get caught up in a cycle of negative words and self-condemnation? If so, what can you do to replace those words with what God says about you?
___
___

Read Romans 8:37, 1 Corinthians 15:57, Colossians 2:10, and Deuteronomy 28:13. How do these passages describe you as a child of God?
___
___

Pray and ask God to make these a reality in your life.

➔ Week 24: God's Special Secrets for You! ✦

The Lord confides in those who fear him; he makes his covenant known to them (Psalm 25:14 AV).

What an awesome thought . . . God confiding in us! As a woman, I love to share with my friends those secret confidences of my heart, and I love to receive those confidences as well. I always know that the people I choose to confide in are ones that can be trusted. Likewise, those that confide in me believe that I too can be trusted. So it delights my heart to know that God trusts us with the knowledge of His covenant and the intimacy of His friendship.

I received several insights from that short but inspiring Scripture. First, I learned that God confides. Just as we share confidences with each other, God divinely shares confidences with us. The secret things belong to the Lord, but there are many things that He alone knows and yet wants us to know. Second, the confidences that He shares are specially designed for those who seek Him and have a relationship with Him. The Scripture says "those who fear him," but it is not the fear that we often think of when something has frightened us. Instead, it is the emotion of being in awe of someone or overwhelmed by the sheer force of that individual's presence and therefore being drawn to him or her to seek out that person. Third, the Scripture clarifies that a covenant exists that is relevant to those He shares it with now. We normally think of the covenant as only being relevant to patriarchs such as Abraham, Isaac, and Jacob. But God's covenant (His binding agreement) is for our generation. And the final insight I received was that since it is God who makes this covenant known and actively pursues telling us about it, He wants us to benefit from it.

Aren't you intrigued when you know that your best friend has a secret that pertains to you? I recall an incident during my college years when my best friend and roommate had a secret about a young man that I had a crush on. While changing classes one day, she called out to me, "Girl, have I got something to tell you about him!" Of course, she had no time to tell me the secret as she rushed on to class, but the expression on her face told me that this boy might possibly like me too. So I waited with great anticipation until we could huddle together later in our dorm room and share the secret that was just for me.

That sense of wonder and excitement that I experienced over a secret about a "silly ole boy" intensifies when I think about the confidences God has in store for me. What about you? Are you wondering with anticipation about the confidences God wants to share with you? Are you thinking of the covenant He wants to make known to you concerning your life? Are you delighted to know that the One who created you actively pursues telling you everything you need to know to live a life of meaning and purpose?

Well if you're like me, you've probably already poured yourself a cup of coffee or a cup of hot tea, grabbed your Bible, pen, and your journal, sat yourself down, and said the words He is longing to hear, "Speak, Lord. I'm listening!"

Week 24 Memory Verse

The Lord confides in those who fear him; he makes his covenant known to them. (Psalm 25:14 AV).

Daily Quiet Reflections

What are some of the secrets that God has whispered to you that you knew were for you only?
___
___

How has being in such intimate fellowship with God affected your life and your other relationships?
___
___

Read Psalm 139. Now focus on verses 16 and 24. How will spending time with God help you to know yourself and your purpose?
___
___

Read Hebrews 10:16-23. What is the covenant mentioned in this passage that God promises to make known to us?
___
___

Because of this covenant, what does God promise to do? (Hint: See verse 17.)
___
___

How does knowing this help you to be confident in your relationship with God?
___
___

↠ Week 25: Divine Plans for You! ↞

But the plans of the Lord stand firm forever, the purposes of His heart through all generations (Psalm 33:11 NIV).

For He spoke and it was done; He commanded, and it stood fast (Psalm 33:9 NAS).

What has God spoken over your life? Jeremiah the prophet conveyed an important message from the heart of God that is meant for each of us. He said, *"For I know the plans I have for you,' declares the Lord, 'plans to prosper you and not to harm you, plans to give you hope and a future'"* (Jeremiah 29:11). The Amplified Version says it this way, *"For I know the thoughts and plans that I have for you, says the Lord, thoughts and plans for welfare and peace and not evil, to give you hope in your final outcome."*

God is thinking about us. He has plans for us—good plans that ensure our welfare. This is great news! Only people that once were without hope truly need hope. Already God knew that we would be in situations that appear hopeless by any definition. He knew that many of us would live our lives with this feeling of hopelessness, and His message declares that there is hope in Him!

Recently, when waiting to have some medical tests run, I sat looking at the other women who, like me, were waiting for various procedures to begin. The results of these procedures could provide answers to what the future would hold. Many of the faces in that waiting room were filled with worry and anxiety. What if the tests were positive? How was life to be different with those results? Would it mean death or life?

As I gazed about the room, I remembered what God had said quietly to my spirit in Jeremiah, and these words meant life to my soul as I accepted the marvelous fact that no matter what the outcome of these tests, my future was bright and filled with hope because the plans of God stand forever. He is not limited by our circumstances. He speaks and it is done.

I wondered if the other women in the room knew this as they waited. I wonder if you know this too. I am not referring to mere head knowledge; do you know in your heart that God thinks about you? Do you know that even in the middle of your current circumstances, the end of the story has not yet been told? Are you trusting in God's promise that His plan has been, is, and will always be to give you hope in your final outcome?

Oh the majesty of God's words! The wonder of His promises to us! We perish when we do not know them or believe them in our hearts.

As I looked at the woman sitting next to me in the waiting room, I felt compelled to say, "Don't worry. It will be okay." Even though the words seemed inadequate, my soul quietly prayed for her that it would indeed be okay. Sometimes, that is the one thing we are required to do—pray.

Week 25 Memory Verse

But the plans of the Lord stand firm forever, the purposes of His heart through all generations (Psalm 33:11).

Daily Quiet Reflections

Read this week's memory verse again. Now review Jeremiah 29:11-13. How do these passages apply to you?
_____
_____

How does knowing that God has a plan for your life help you to live a life filled with purpose?
_____
_____

What are some ways that God has confirmed in His Word through wise counsel, or through your gifts and talents, the purpose you may be called to fulfill?
_____
_____

What doors have closed to you that have given you an indication that some paths were not meant for you to pursue?
_____
_____

What doors are opening that may be an indication of a path that God may be calling you to for this season of your life?
_____
_____

The Bible says that when He opens doors no one will be able to close them; when He closes doors no one will be able to open them (Isaiah 22:22). What impact does this passage have on circumstances that may be impacting your ability to pursue the plans you believe God has for you?
_____
_____

➜ WEEK 26: HOW YOU SEE YOURSELF MATTERS! ⬅

The other day while watching the news, I saw a comical sight. A 350 pound black bear cub was at the top of a very tall pine tree, and at the bottom of the tree sat the culprit that had sent the bear running up the tree in the first place—a small, nine pound cat! The cat had an expression on its face that seemed to say, "And I better not catch you in my yard again!"

Later, when animal specialists were asked why the bear cub was so afraid of the cat and why the cat wasn't afraid of the bear cub, the specialists responded that neither of them is aware of their size. The bear didn't realize he could beat the tar out of that cat, and the cat didn't realize that had the bear known this, she would have been in danger of losing one of her nine lives! Neither animal knew his true size or power, and so the brave cat was at an advantage. She could bully that bear, and that bear was terrified.

Life is a lot like that in the spiritual realm. God has given those of us in Christ authority and power over our enemy the devil. Even though Satan is described in Scripture as a roaring lion, that's all he is—a roaring loan. His teeth and claws have been removed, and he is powerless against the spirit of God that resides in a believer. Because he has no power over us, his bark is literally bigger than his bite. He is similar to that cat in that he struts around and carries on something furious, causing many believers to head for the hills or up a tree. Like the bear, we seem unaware that we have more power and might than our enemy because we have the God of the universe on our side.

We are shaken up by Satan's roar and therefore never challenge him with the authority and power given us. Don't get me wrong, when the economy is in shambles, people are losing their homes and jobs, and everything seems out of control, it can be pretty frightening! But if we could only see the bigness of our God and His sovereignty over our circumstances, we would not lose hope. In the spiritual realm, this looks as ridiculous as that big 350 pound bear looked while clinging to that pine tree, too afraid to come down because of a nine pound cat! If we could only remove those spiritual blinders from our eyes, then we could see what God sees in us when He looks at the affairs on earth. We are mighty warriors, princes or princesses, sons or daughters of the Most High God. We have no need to be afraid of any power of the enemy but must take our rightful place as heirs of God.

Finally, be strong in the Lord and in his mighty power. Put on the full armor of God so that you can take your stand against the devil's schemes (Ephesians 6:10-11 NIV).

Now, come down out of that tree! Remember, the devil is only a nine pound cat!

Week 26 Memory Verse

Finally, be strong in the Lord and in his mighty power. Put on the full armor of God so that you can take your stand against the devil's schemes (Ephesians 6:10-11 NIV).

Daily Quiet Reflections

What are some of the ways that your vision of yourself has not been consistent with how God sees you?

_____
_____

List some of the passages of Scripture that provide you with God's view of who you are.

_____
_____

Identify three characteristics that you know are special for you.

_____
_____

How can you use your uniqueness to glorify God?

_____
_____

What have been some obstacles in your past that God has helped you to overcome?

_____
_____

How does remembering past victories give you strength for today's battles?

_____
_____

→ Week 27: Sowing and Reaping ←

There are so many great business principles in the Bible that teach us about leadership, service, building relationships, and fair dealing. Because this is true, I am beginning to look at these principles with new eyes as I manage my own business. For example, yesterday, I read a passage of Scripture that reinforced how to grow a business. It said, *"They sowed fields and planted vineyards that yielded a fruitful harvest; He blessed them and their numbers greatly increased, and He did not let their herds diminish"* (Psalm 107:37-38 NIV).

At first glance, you may be tempted to ask, "What do vineyards and herds have to do with running a business?" To my way of thinking, a lot! The principle of sowing and reaping is a core business principle. It is also a core life principle. You've heard it said that you will only get out of it what you put into it. This is true in business, in relationships, and in any worthwhile endeavor. If I sow my time, money, talent, and creativity into my business, I should expect a harvest that produces more business and more opportunities to serve my clients.

But a factor that I wouldn't want you to miss is the role God plays in all of this. Notice it says, "He blessed them . . . He did not let their herds diminish." Naturally, this means that we must first do our part by sowing, planting, and watering; but the increase comes from God. Just as He plays a role in the universal concept of sowing and reaping in nature, the same is true as we apply this principle to our businesses and other endeavors. We must roll up our sleeves and work diligently, but it is God that provides the increase in our clients, the favor given to our products, and the boost to our sales. Anyone who really believes that they achieved success all by themselves have merely fooled themselves into believing they have control over their own heartbeats and are the suppliers of the air that they breathe.

As you begin to plan your day, don't only focus on the challenging work ahead but get energized thinking of the reward that is sure to come when you do all that you can in the natural, trusting God to produce supernatural results!

Week 27 Memory Verse

They sowed fields and planted fields that yielded a fruitful harvest. He blessed them and their numbers greatly increased and He did not let their herds diminish (Psalm 107:37-38 NIV).

Daily Quiet Reflections

What are some of the "fields" that you are planting into now and from which you are awaiting a harvest?
_____
_____

What has been the most difficult part of the planting season?
_____
_____

What has God taught you about the important of patience in waiting your harvest?
_____
_____

What are some useful steps that you can take to ensure that the harvest you receive is a fruitful one?
_____
_____

If you have not had a productive planting season, what can you do to correct that going forward?
_____
_____

How does the principle of sowing and reaping work in the areas of your relationships? In your business? In your ministry?
_____
_____

⇾ Week 28: Choose To Be Content ⇽

We are never going to be fully content in life until we choose to be content. There will always be something else we are searching for unless we stop, take note of our lives, and declare, "I am content." What I've come to realize is that contentment is a choice we make each day. We can look for all that is missing in our lives and dwell on it, or we can look at all that we have in our lives and dwell on that. In doing the latter, we come to realize that our lives are rich and full, although not without difficulty for that is part of the journey. For what would a truly rich life be if there were no hardships, no disappointments, and no regrets? Bland and flavorless, I imagine. Our challenges, along with the happy times, the joyful events, and the winning moments, give life texture, intrigue, and adventure.

This realization hit me as I started a new chapter of my life—that of the empty nester. Why didn't anyone tell me how lonely I would be? Where were the warning signals that a big loss was about to occur? I went along haplessly during the days before my daughter's departure for college, thinking I had it all together. After she left, I found myself completely undone and wondered how I would enjoy my life in this very quiet, empty nest.

Some said, "I tried to tell you what it would be like." And that of course is true. All my empty nester friends did send out a few SOS's, but I was still clueless. Others said, "You have your work; you'll get over it." And although that may be true, work will never take the place of my girl; in fact, it doesn't even come close.

So, as is typical of me, I went to God's Word to gain comfort and guidance. And as is so typical of Him, He spoke to me gently through the words of the prophet Isaiah: *"If you do not stand in your faith, you will not stand at all"* (Isaiah 7:9 NIV). That is wise counsel.

I took it to mean that sometimes we simply have to "faith it" until we make it. Even when your world feels upside down, you must choose to believe that better days are ahead and that the plans of God are still being worked out on your behalf. In other words, you must choose to be content now no matter what the circumstances. And that is what I have chosen to be—content.

Do I wish that for a moment I could turn back time and still be able to push my little girl on her swing? Sometimes. But more than that, I look forward to the bright future that is ahead for all of us. What adventure! What joy!

Yes, today I choose to be content, and with God's help I will make this same choice tomorrow and the day after that and the day after that . . .

> *I am not saying this because I am in need, for I have learned to be content whatever the circumstances. I know what it is to be in need, and I know what it is to have plenty. I have learned the secret of being content in any and every situation, whether well fed or hungry, whether living in plenty or in want. I can do everything through him who gives me strength* (Philippians 4:11-13).

Week 28 Memory Verse

For I have learned to be content whatever the circumstances (Philippians 4:11 NIV).

Daily Quiet Reflections

Read Philippians 4:1-13. Describe in your own words what you believe the passage is saying.
_____
_____

How does this apply to your life?
_____
_____

What can you do to learn to be content despite your circumstances?
_____
_____

What promise does God make in this passage that will help you in making the choice to be content daily?
_____
_____

What are some examples from your life that confirm that you can do all things through Christ?
_____
_____

Pray that no matter what your circumstances are today, God will provide you with a heart of contentment.

☙ Week 29: Waiting on Something New ❧

Is God doing a new thing in your life?

I was preparing for a business trip to New York recently. Despite my best efforts to maintain my peace, I was feeling anxious about it because I knew I would meet with people that are so out of my league that I wondered what on earth caused me to agree to go in the first place. I knew I was going because it was a "God thing," but the whole time I had been praying, *Lord, what am I supposed to say? How am I to conduct myself with this group?* In other words, *What's the plan?* Then I sat and listened. Nothing.

The next day I went through the same routine. *Lord, I need your help. How do I prepare effectively?* Still nothing.

As the days went by and the trip got closer, I began to panic and started trying to devise my own plan. But somehow, my attempts seemed lame and disconnected. I didn't feel the same level of confidence I normally would, and that was so frustrating! Finally, one afternoon while driving to an engagement, I let out one word, "Help!" As my eyes darted up to heaven and then back to the traffic, I knew God knew I was talking to Him. Now, don't misunderstand me. I'm always sure that God speaks in His own way and in His own time. I'm just sometimes very concerned that in my agitation, I don't always listen too well, and I didn't want to miss anything He might have said. I knew I needed to be still and stop being so impatient, but I was running out of time!

The next morning in my quiet time with God, I read a passage of Scripture that arrested my attention:

> *Forget the former things; do not dwell on the past. See I am doing a new thing! Now it springs up; do you not perceive it? I am making a way in the desert and streams in the wasteland* (Isaiah 43:18-19 NIV).

Now this was getting interesting!

Imagine that . . . God is doing a new thing! He remains the same with all His power and glory, but His creative nature is not fully revealed. There is even more of Him to learn about and know. That thought excited me as I thought about my own circumstances and wondered what new thing He was about to do. And yes, I am waiting for more revelation, but I am delighted to know that He is up to something new as far as I'm concerned.

Now I want to let you in on a little secret: He is up to something as far as you are concerned too! It is something new. He is making a way in your desert and streams in your wasteland. Do you not perceive it?

So forget the former things, whatever it is that has kept you dwelling in the past—possibly dwelling on old solutions to new problems or thinking about past mistakes that keep you from moving forward to redemption. Perhaps, like me, God has placed you out of your league on purpose so that you can learn a new way of doing things. Or maybe He wants to do something new in your marriage, your relationships, your work, or your ministry. Whatever it is, start looking for the new things God is ready to do through you. I'm planning too, because I know if we will only receive it, He is willing to take us to a higher place on our journey. I want to keep growing and moving to this higher place. Don't you?

Week 29 Memory Verse

Behold, I am doing a new thing, can you not perceive it? (Isaiah 43:19 NIV)

Daily Quiet Reflections

Describe some times when God has begun a new work in your life. What did it feel like?

_____
_____

What was your biggest concern about being out of your comfort zone, and how did God respond to your concerns?

_____
_____

What are you learning from those times when God begins to do a new work in your life?

_____
_____

If you still have concerns about the current new thing God is doing, make a list of them and take them to God in prayer. Chart His response over the next several weeks.

_____
_____

If God has provided you with clarity around some new things that He is working out in your relationships, your work, your business, etc., write down some action items that you believe could move you in the direction God is moving in your life.

_____
_____

Pray over your action list and ask God to confirm this direction either through His Word, through godly counsel, or both.

⇥ Week 30: Is It Raining in Someone's Life? ⇤

It's been raining a lot this past week in my hometown, and I have loved it. Usually a rainy day can spoil everything—if you have plans. But that was just it; I didn't have any plans. I wasn't getting on an airplane this week, I didn't have any outside activities to attend, and the rain saved me the chore of watering my grass. I guess if any of those circumstances had been different, I would have been prone to whine about the rain as I normally would if my plans were being interrupted.

I think the same frame of mind is true in spiritual matters as well. We are often completely oblivious to the rain that occurs in life if it doesn't affect us or change our plans. If you think about it, it's raining for those parents that have a son or daughter serving in the armed forces right now in danger every day. It's raining for those children starving in Third World countries with no hope for food. And it's raining for those people who have never known the Messiah or are completely unaware that God loves them. In all these cases, a downpour has occurred, and living life uninterrupted and in abundance seems a distant dream. They long for the sun and are desperate for a brighter day.

But many of us, me included, seem completely unaware of their plight since that "rain" is not affecting our plans or us. I can't help but think that God must be saddened as we "splash" off to our worship services but refuse to speak to our next door neighbor who doesn't know God loves them. Surely His heart must break as we attend another great religious conference but give no thought to sharing the good news of the gospel with those we work with every day. Yes, many times we are simply enjoying the rain from inside our comfortable lives, not knowing that someone else is out there in that storm searching for a safe harbor.

I am reminded of a Scripture spoken by the prophet Isaiah:

The Sovereign Lord has given me an instructed tongue, to know the word that sustains the weary. He wakens me morning by morning, wakens my ear to listen like one being taught. The Sovereign Lord has opened my ears, and I have not been rebellious, I have not drawn back (Isaiah 50:4-5 NIV).

I think God is opening our ears to hear the rain all around us in the lives of others. I would encourage each of us, if we hear His voice, to agree not to harden our hearts.

Week 30 Memory Verse

The Sovereign Lord has given me an instructed tongue, to know the word that sustains the weary. He wakens me morning by morning, wakens my ear to listen like one being taught. The Sovereign Lord has opened my ears, and I have not been rebellious, I have not drawn back (Isaiah 50:4-5 NIV).

Daily Quiet Reflections

Read this week's memory verse again. What does it mean to be given "an instructed tongue, to know the word that sustains the weary"?
_____
_____

Who are the people in your circle of influence that may need an encouraging word or some help that you can provide?
_____
_____

What is one thing you can do to reach out to the people whom God has placed in your path that may need to be refreshed?
_____
_____

Read Matthew 25:40. How does this apply to you?
_____
_____

Who are some of the "least of these"?
_____
_____

Spend time praying that God will show you someone who is going through a rainy season and ask that He provide you with the right way to help him or her.

➜ Week 31: Walking by Faith ⇠

I've been grappling with something recently, the issue of walking by faith and not by sight. I thought I was doing that rather well, and to some degree I have been; but just when I think I have it all figured out, some new faith walk test comes my way. Then I feel like a beginner again and not the seasoned faith walker that I am.

Not so long ago, a faith test came in the form of trusting God with a new business venture. I've always been fortunate enough to have had a career that allowed me to have plenty of resources. Whatever I needed to get the job done was readily available in a big company environment. If I needed supplies, I ordered them. If I needed technical support, I picked up the phone and someone took care of it. Airline reservations needed? Done! And of course, due to the nature of my work, getting new clients was no challenge while I worked for a large corporation. I guess you could say I had it made. But then, at God's leading, I decided to move out in faith and start something completely new and different with Him.

To say that it was an adventure would be an understatement! While certainly I was having the time of my life, I also had some anxious moments. Most of those revolved around the entire issue of resources and having the faith to believe that God truly will provide all my needs according to His riches in Christ Jesus.

I decided to have a talk with Him, a small business meeting to discuss the issue of resources and how I was feeling just a tiny bit stressed with all that needed to be done in my office. And that's when the entire discussion around walking by faith and not by sight came up as God reminded me through His Word of how completely aware He is of all our needs. This is what He said,

> *Walk out into the fields and look at the wildflowers. They never primp or shop, but have you ever seen color and design quite like it? The ten best-dressed men and women in the country look shabby alongside them. If God gives such attention to the appear-*

ance of wildflowers—most of which are never even seen—don't you think he'll attend to you, take pride in you, do his best for you? What I'm trying to do here is to get you to relax and don't be so preoccupied with getting so that you can respond to God's giving. People who don't know God and the way he works fuss over these things, but you know both God and how he works. Steep your life in God-reality, God-initiative, and God-provisions. Don't worry about missing out. You'll find all your everyday human concerns will be met (Matthew 6:28-34 MSG).

And with that, our business meeting was over, and we had covered everything on the agenda. God is very efficient that way.

I found this reminder very comforting as I remembered that you and I are much more important to God than flowers or any other living creature. And of course, He knows exactly what we need. Whether it is resources for a new business venture or peace for our souls, He is the ultimate provider.

So if you are struggling with some issue today that is requiring you to trust God's good intentions toward you rather than trusting what you may see in your circumstances (commonly known as walking by faith and not by sight issues), then schedule some time to meet with Him. He invites us to *"come and let us discuss this"* (Isaiah 1:18 HCSB). I believe you will find the very answers you are looking for and reassurance that it is going to be okay.

Week 31 Memory Verse

Ask and it will be given to you; seek and you will find; knock and the door will be opened to you (Matthew 7:7 NIV).

Daily Quiet Reflections

Read this week's memory verse again. How does this apply to walking by faith and not by sight?
___
___

When you pray and get no desired result, does it mean that you prayed for the wrong thing? Explain your answer.
___
___

When all aspects of life seems to be out of your control, what choices do you have?
___
___

In what ways do you need God for your resources?
___
___

What specific things or outcomes are you trusting God for in your present circumstances?
___
___

What is it about God that lets you know that He is real and that He cares about what concerns you?
___
___

Week 32: The Truth About Who You Are

Have you ever felt really tired of living a defeated life? Have you ever wondered why your life of faith seems to be less than you had hoped it would be? Are you still asking yourself, *Where is the victory I am supposed to be experiencing?* I have gone through what I call my "sick and tired" seasons, and I have learned over time that the abundant life that God desires for us doesn't happen if we are not willing to seize it with everything in us.

When I was in college, students could audit classes. This meant that you could attend the class and obtain all the information provided, but you didn't have to do any homework or take any tests. Of course, you didn't receive a grade for audited classes, but the benefit was that you could try out the class to see if you liked it without any risks (like receiving a bad grade if the class was really difficult). The down side was that you never knew whether you had actually learned any of the key concepts because your knowledge was never put to the test.

Many times we go through our life's journey with God as though we are auditing a course. It begins with our salvation in Christ, where we know we have the security of eternal life. But for many of us, we miss knowing what true liberty in Christ really means. We are waiting for God to zap us into all that we are in Christ. We want the liberty God has promised to just wash over us and overtake us. We become disappointed when life continues to be difficult or is not as fulfilling as we had hoped it would be. The supernatural transformation of our lives has already occurred when we have a right relationship with God and are walking in fellowship with Him through His Son. We are liberated, we are victorious, and we have the power of the living God on the inside of us! So why doesn't it always feel as though we do?

The reason is because we may be accepting those subtle lies that the enemy of our souls quite often whispers to us. This may manifest in words such as, *If God is as great as you think He is, why can't He just cause you to be who you are in Christ supernaturally?"* Or *Maybe this liberty in Christ stuff isn't real. If it is, why are you still struggling to live victoriously after being saved so long?* Perhaps the enemy has even used Scripture to convince you that who you are in Christ will never happen: "He who the Son sets free is free indeed." *But you're not free; you're still having the same powerless life, so maybe there really is no power in Jesus?*

Satan has used that strategy for centuries. He even used it with Jesus (Luke 4:9-11). But just as Jesus did, we must always respond with the truth of God's Word. The truth is, faith without works is dead. We must each be willing to walk out our faith. We don't do this to save ourselves; instead, we do it to mature and to become what we already are in Christ. The supernatural work of God has already been done. Yes, He could zap us into instant victory, but how would we then know His power if we had never had to deal with those strongholds (anything that keeps us from living a liberated life) that are clearly more than our human power can handle?

We begin to know God through the discipleship process. Through our journey with Him, we see His glory revealed in our lives. You and I will never know who we are in Christ until we see God work, powerfully removing the strongholds in our lives that keep us from walking in full liberty. This requires our full attention and a great deal of effort and energy. To illustrate this point, I am reminded of a time when one of my clients thought she had charged up her cell phone because she had connected it to the phone charger. She realized later that she had neglected to plug the charger into the power source. As a result, the cell phone was dead and depleted of any ability to receive calls. The phone and the charger were both equipped to do their jobs, but neither could do what they were created to do without their source of power.

The same is true for us. We will never be all that we were created to be without God's power. If we are in Christ, then we have the power source living on the inside of us; but we must "plug in." Just as the cell phone is not able to do anything it was designed to do without staying powered up, this holds true for you and me. We plug into our source of power by spending time with God—reading His Word, meditating, seeking fellowship with other believers, and attending worship services. We consciously decide to refute those lies that keep us from having victory and replace those lies with truth. We surround ourselves with worship music and get into the holy habit of praise! All of these can keep us plugged into the source of all our power. With this comes liberty!

If you want to have a life of victory, if you want to enjoy freedom from anything that keeps you from becoming all that God intended you to be, then stop auditing your life and get to work. And don't be afraid of the tests. Know that He who has begun a good work in you will complete it just as He said He would.

Week 32 Memory Verse

Being confident of this, that He who began a good work in you will carry it on to completion until the day of Christ Jesus (Philippians 1:6 NIV).

Daily Quiet Reflections

What is there that transforms us when we accept Christ into our lives?
___
___

What do you believe is the good work being referred to in the memory verse?
___
___

How can knowing about this good work help you to walk in victory?
___
___

What do you believe you need in your life in order to experience the victory promised in God's Word?
___
___

Write a prayer to God asking for evidence of victory in the parts of your life that seem defeated.
___
___

Romans 4:17 says God is "the God who gives life to the dead, and calls things that are not as though they were." How can this passage be applied to you today?
___
___

↛ Week 33: God Can Do What Even Oprah Can't ↚

Not so long ago, the world news was making much over the opening of Oprah Winfrey's forty million dollar school for girls in South Africa. This benevolence was wonderful and a great example of giving. On CNN, Oprah shared the story of how she expressed a desire to see each little girl grow up and have the opportunity to go to college. Upon making this known, one little girl asked, "But who will pay for that?" Oprah responded, "I will," to which the little girl dropped her head into her hands and begin to cry. Puzzled by this response, Oprah asked her, "Why are you crying?" The girl replied, "I am crying at the thought of it."

That touched me so deeply. Here this little girl was weeping at the thought of what was already planned for her based on a promise made by a woman that she barely knew. I understood this great emotion. All one has to do to understand the feelings of this young girl is to sit quietly and read just one or two promises found in the Word of God to be shaken to the core with emotion. Oh, if we could only grasp and receive into our hearts the promises of God in this same way! If we could really take what He says in Jeremiah 29:11 *("For I know the plans I have for you, says the Lord, plans for good and not catastrophe, plans for a great future and an eternal hope")* and perceive it in such a manner that it caused us to pause in awesome wonder. If we could began to allow this promise to sink into our spirits, the true meaning of those words and their application would become real in our lives.

What if we really accepted the promise of God that says, *"No eye has seen, no ear has heard, no mind has conceived what God has prepared for those who love Him"* (1 Corinthians 2:9; Isaiah 64:4)? What would our attitudes and actions be as we went through each day with the mere thought of this going over and over in our minds? If we were to do that and meditate on the magnificence of these promises, we too would drop our heads into our hands and weep at the thought of it.

I encourage each of us to take some time to reflect on the many promises of God for us and learn to accept the fact that they are true and will happen. For He has promised that He will fulfill His purpose for us, and He will not abandon the work of His hands (Psalm 138:8). Some of these promises may seem to be in the distant future. Whether they are a promise for today or in the future, they have already been prepared. They are already planned out and we can trust in the One who has committed to do everything He promised. I think when we ponder on God's promises for any period of time at all, our response will be like that of the little girl in South Africa. And when asked by our Father, "Little one, why are you crying?" with our faces in our hands, with great gratitude and emotion we will say, "I am crying at the mere thought of it."

Week 33 Memory Verse

No eye has seen, no ear has heard, no mind has conceived what God has prepared for those who love Him (1 Corinthians 2:9 NIV).

Daily Quiet Reflections

This week's memory verse contains an amazing promise. What do you believe God has prepared for you?
___
___

Read Matthew 6:25-34, John 10:10, John 15:11, Galatians 5:1, and Colossians 3:15. What are some things that God has already promised and prepared for you?
___
___

What are the parts of your life you take for granted?
___
___

What are some of the blessings in your life?
___
___

Is there any circumstance in your life that you believe may be too difficult for God to handle?
___
___

What is keeping you from really trusting God today?
___
___

➢ Week 34: No More Window Shopping ➣

Like most women, I love to shop for new things! Actually, I like shopping for old things too. I especially love shopping online because I can shop from the comfort of my home wearing my fluffy slippers. Whether it is to buy something to adorn my home, or for a gift for a loved one, or something just for me, it's always fun to shop! However, I have never been very fond of window shopping—going to the mall just to look. I've never quite understood that concept. I mean, what's the point of shopping if you are not going to buy anything? To me that would be the equivalent of going fishing with no goal of catching a fish. Any self-respecting fisherman gets on their boat with the idea that they are coming home with some fish. So when I go shopping, I intend to come home with something!

However, many times we approach God's Word as though we are on a window shopping trip. We see a powerful verse in the Scripture such as, "Treat others as you would like to be treated" and we think, *Isn't that a lovely verse, so powerful and so right.* Or we may read, "Love others as I have loved you" and we think, *I wish everyone would do that.* We go shopping through the Bible, looking at all the pretty verses and commenting on their goodness and rightness but never "buying" any of them into our lives.

Wouldn't it be something if we got serious about our shopping trip through the Bible? What would happen if we determined that we wouldn't come home the same way we left? What if we acquired something in God's Word just for ourselves and allowed it to change our lives?

When we walk through the pages of Scripture without applying anything that we read to our lives, we've just gone on a window shopping trip. If you're like me, you're still trying to figure out what the fun is in that.

God invites us on a shopping trip designed specifically for us. Everything there was designed with us in mind. Everything is just our size and shows off our figures better than anything we've ever worn. It is all in the color we love. And we look fabulous wearing it!

Where can we find this amazing place? In the pages of His Word—the Bible!

Remember, no more window shopping! Let's shop until we drop, and let's bring it all home!

Week 34 Memory Verse

May the God of hope fill you with all joy and peace as you trust in Him, so that you may overflow with hope by the power of the Holy Spirit (Romans 15:13 NIV).

Daily Quiet Reflections

Based on the memory verse, what must you to do to be filled with joy and peace?
_____
_____

How can taking this passage (Romans 15:13) and making it your own improve your life?
_____
_____

What are some passages of Scripture that you know but have never really applied the truth of them in your own life?
_____
_____

If your past was filled with pain or trauma, to whom do you look for hope in a great tomorrow?
_____
_____

If there is something about yourself that needs to change, what can you and God do together to change it?
_____
_____

Is it more productive for you to look back or look ahead? Why?
_____
_____

➸ Week 35: Have You Lost Your Way? ✦

Have you ever gotten lost? If you have, you know that it can be a frightening experience, or at least one that causes great anxiety.

I became lost once while traveling by car to another city to meet with a client. Initially, I didn't know I was lost because I had received directions from my client and thought that if anyone would know how to get to his office, he would. *Wrong!* As I was driving along, it suddenly occurred to me that I was leaving the city and entering the countryside. The only thing I knew for sure was that his office was in the city. I rechecked the directions he had given me and confirmed that I had followed all his instructions perfectly. But still I knew something wasn't right, and that's when a little panic arrived. I was able to contact him by cell phone, and that's when we discovered that he had told me to go south when I should have gone north. By then I had driven several miles in the wrong direction and had added an additional thirty minutes to my driving time.

That was easily corrected, but greater truths begin to emerge from that incident. How often have we gone the wrong way because we've relied on faulty directions in our lives? How many times have we made important decisions based on the counsel of an unwise person? Or how many times have we made choices in life that we soon regretted because we didn't have the right information? I'm sure all of us could look back on some circumstances in our lives and say, "If I had only known then what I know now, I would have done things so differently."

It's times like these when we come to value the importance of getting our directions in life from the right source. You see, when we solely rely on others or ourselves for the right directions, we run the great risk of going the wrong way because we don't have the right map. On the other hand, when we go to the One who knows all and sees all—the One who has the correct road map—then we know our chances of getting lost are impossible.

We have a significant promise from God, one that assures His children that He will always accompany them on their journeys in life no matter where it may lead. Here's how He says it:

Fear not, for I have redeemed you; I have summoned you by name; you are mine. When you pass through the waters, I will be with you; and when you pass through the rivers, they will not sweep over you. When you walk through the fire, you will not be burned; the flames will not set you ablaze . . . since you are precious and honored in my sight and because I love you (Isaiah 43:1-2,4 NIV).

Now that's a great promise!

Are you feeling lost today? Then, go to the One who created you and ask Him for direction. He has the right map, He will never leave you, and He will show you the right way. Why? Because you are precious to Him, and He loves you.

Week 35 Memory Verse

Fear not, for I have redeemed you; I have summoned you by name; you are mine. When you pass through the waters, I will be with you (Isaiah 43:1).

Daily Quiet Reflections

What does it mean to you to know that you have been redeemed and summoned by name?
___
___

Why do you think God starts off by saying, "Fear not"?
___
___

How does knowing that God has promised to be with you help in your daily life?
___
___

What is one way that you can remind yourself of the truth of the promise found in Isaiah 43:1-2, 4)?
___
___

What road are you on today?
___
___

How can you be sure that you are going in the right direction?
___
___

⇥ Week 36: Your Rainbow of Hope ⇤

I have always had a great fondness for rainbows. I'm not sure why, but I suspect that part of it may be the brilliance of the colors. Or maybe it's the complexity of their formulation that captivates my fascination. But more than these, I like what rainbows symbolize. They symbolize a covenant between the Creator and His creation. This covenant was established during the days of Noah when God said, *"This bow is the sign of the covenant I have established between Me and all life on the earth"* (Genesis 9:17). But what exactly does this covenant mean? The covenant referred to was God's promise that He would never again allow the earth to be completely destroyed by water.

What an important promise to make because prior to the first flood, while Noah was still building the ark, no one had ever seen rain before. That is why Noah's generation never believed his predictions about the oncoming flood or the need for an ark. They had no proof of rain's existence until after it came. As a result, after the flood, God's covenant—in the form of a rainbow—kept mankind from being terrified at the sight of a cloud because they knew that God had promised that rain would not result in total disaster.

That's true in life too. We have often heard that into every life a little rain must fall. We are all faced with circumstances that could strike terror into our hearts and cause us to wonder if we will be destroyed. Whether it is the loss of a loved one, a child gone astray, an ending of a relationship, or a business deal gone bad, all troubling circumstances have the capability of creating fear and sorrow that could be never ending until we remember God's rainbow promise to us.

> *Beloved, consider it pure joy whenever you face trials of many kinds, because you know that the testing of your faith develops perseverance. Perseverance must finish its work so that you may be mature and complete, not lacking anything* (James 1:3-4).

Just as the rain in nature cause the growth of many living creatures and plants, so too does the rain that occurs in our lives. It creates perseverance and wisdom, and teaches us to stand firm as we see the promises of God come to life in our circumstances. Just as the rainbow appears in the sky after a storm, so too will the covenant of God's promises appear in the fabric of a life totally surrendered to Him. Rainbows don't appear before the storm. Their reassuring presence is only manifested as the clouds begin to clear.

If you are in the middle of one of life's storms, and the flood waters seem as though they will engulf you, you can be sure of one thing—God's covenant with you. Watch carefully for it. One day when you may least expect it, a brilliant, colorful ray will begin to form on the horizon, and you will hear God's voice in the gentle breeze whispering, *"I, myself do establish my covenant with you . . . never again will the waters become a flood to destroy all life"* (Genesis 9:9,15 NIV).

Week 36 Memory Verse

Beloved, consider it pure joy whenever you face trials of many kinds, because you know that the testing of your faith develops perseverance. Perseverance must finish its work so that you may be mature and complete, not lacking anything (James 1:3-4).

Daily Quiet Reflections

Is it really possible to have joy or to laugh in the face of adversity? If so, how?
_____
_____

What are some of the benefits God lists as a result of the trials we face?
_____
_____

What does it mean to not lack anything?
_____
_____

Has God ever done anything in your life that cannot be explained?
_____
_____

When you pray and there is silence from God, does it mean that He is not listening to you?
_____
_____

What is there about God that reaches you when you are going through a difficult trial of faith?
_____
_____

⇝ Week 37: Time in God's Waiting Room ⇜

So Pharaoh sent for Joseph, and he was quickly brought from the dungeon (Genesis 41:14).

Imagine what that day was like for Joseph! It had been two years since God had used him to interpret the dreams of the chief baker and the chief cupbearer from Pharaoh's staff. Two years had passed since he had hoped that this connection would create an opportunity to get him out of jail. He spent two years wondering why no one had remembered him. Two years had gone by to think about the dream God had placed in his heart and to wonder if maybe he had gotten it wrong or had misunderstood. And then one day, a day like hundreds of days before, Pharaoh sent for him. Can you imagine it? How his heart must have beat with anticipation. What had happened? Why was Pharaoh sending for him out of the blue? What had he done? Was he in trouble? Was he to be finally free at last?

Think of the moment Joseph was brought out of the dungeon. He had no way of knowing what the outcome would be that day. He didn't know if his being called was a good thing or a bad thing. However, the next part of the passage is very revealing. It says, "But Joseph first shaved himself, changed his clothes, and made himself presentable; then he came into Pharaoh's presence." In other words, Joseph got ready. Even though he wasn't sure why he was being pulled out of the dungeon to meet with Pharaoh, he wanted to be sure that Pharaoh's first impression of him was a good one.

What an important life principle. Many times we too are in "God's waiting room." The waiting room may feel like a dungeon—dark, empty, useless, and hopeless. The dungeon is the place and season in our lives that seem as though nothing is happening. The dreams we had for our lives seem impossible in the dungeon or have died altogether. It is in the dungeon that we wonder if we are forgotten by those significant to us and especially by God. The dungeon stay seems endless and forever; day after day is the same, and the question in our heart is *How long, God?* Or *God, have you forgotten about me?*

But then one day everything changes. Suddenly, our circumstances are turned upside down, and doors that were closed and locked before are opened in a way that amaze us and literally take our breath away! We know in that instant that no one could have opened the door to our dungeon but God. What will be our response? Will we flee from the dungeon in our old "dungeon clothes" or will we, like Joseph, stop to prepare ourselves for the opportunity awaiting us?

If you are in that season of waiting, be encouraged. This season didn't come to stay. It came to pass. And when it does, be ready. Use your "dungeon days" to seek God and know His heart. Spend time with Him and read His Word because one day soon, the door will open, and you will be brought out quickly. Who knows, it could be today!

Week 37 Memory Verse

When the Lord brought back his exiles to Jerusalem, it was like a dream! We were filled with laughter, and we sang for joy. And the other nations said, "What amazing things the Lord has done for them." Yes, the Lord has done amazing things for us! What joy! (Psalm 126:1-3).

Daily Quiet Reflections

Where is God when it seems as though He has abandoned you and left you alone in His waiting room?
___
___

How does spending time in God's waiting room help you to become the person God intends for you to be?
___
___

Proverbs 3:3-7 tells us in part that we must trust in God even when we don't understand what He is doing. What else does this passage say?
___
___

What can you do to apply this passage to your life?
___
___

Have you ever come out of a season of waiting and felt as the people of Israel did in the memory verse passage? Describe the event here.
___
___

How can you seek God with all your heart during a season of waiting?
___
___

➳ Week 38: God Wants Us To Win! ↞

I press on toward the goal to win the [supreme and heavenly] prize to which God in Christ Jesus is calling us upward (Philippians 3:14 AMP).

It's pageant season at my house. As many of my friends will attest, I have resisted becoming a "pageant mom" from the beginning. Why? Because I thought it was synonymous with "cheerleader mom" or "soccer mom." I had visions of women going off the deep end when their kids didn't win. So I wasn't going to let these pageants get to me. I must admit, though, after my daughter won her first crown, suddenly winning the next crown became a magnificent obsession! Who can resist the planning that goes into a competition? I enjoyed selecting the competition wardrobe, going to photo shoots for the perfect picture, getting fitted in the evening gown that is sure to wow the judges, soliciting sponsors, checking out the other competition, and on and on. Actually, I don't have much time for my life right now because I am officially a "pageant mom"!

Something happened the other day while I was having a quiet time with the Lord. I was telling Him for the one hundredth time all the reasons I thought my girl deserved to win her next big pageant. Suddenly I felt ridiculous bothering God with such a trivial matter when I knew He had to deal with more complicated, important issues like world peace. Just as that thought entered my head, another thought came to me with greater force and caused me to stop and reflect on who God is. In His still, quiet voice, God seemed to say to me, "I love the way you love your girl and will do everything you can to help her. It is exactly the way I feel about my children. It is exactly the way I feel about you."

Whoa! Here I was being tempted to think that my concerns and desires as a mother weren't important to God, when I realized that simply wasn't true. In fact, the more I thought about my behavior over these past few weeks, the more I realized that God's desire for

His children is exactly the same—He wants us to win! Obviously, we're not competing in a pageant, but we are in the greatest battle that ever existed. This battle started in the garden of Eden—the battle between right and wrong, good and evil, death and life. And God wants us to win! He says in Philippians 1:7, "*It is right for me to feel this way about you because I have you in my heart.*" What way does God feel about us? The way you feel about anyone you love with your entire being. This feeling says, "I want the best for you; I want you to succeed; and I want your future to be bright because I want you to have victory in your life!"

What a thought! And isn't it true? God says, *"I will not forget you. Behold, I have indelibly imprinted (tattooed a picture of) you on the palm of each of My hands"* (Isaiah 49:16 AMP). Our faces are constantly before Him. God is constantly thinking about us. He continually has us on His mind. In fact, He has so many thoughts about us, they outnumber the sand (Psalm 139:17-18). We are His magnificent obsession!

So if you see me behaving a bit like a pageant mom with my daughter these days, don't worry. I have it under control. It just serves as a tiny reminder to me of the way God feels about you and me.

Week 38 Memory Verse

I will not forget you. Behold, I have indelibly imprinted you on the palm of each of My hands (Isaiah 49:15-16).

Daily Quiet Reflections

What evidence do you have that God wants you to live a victorious life?
___
___

How does knowing that God has you imprinted or tattooed on the palm of His hands impact you?
___
___

How do we go from a mindset of losing to a mindset of winning?
___
___

How can you come to know the victorious life God has planned for you?
___
___

Read Romans 7:14-25. What does the apostle Paul say is the secret to a victorious life in Christ?
___
___

What is one thing you can do today that will move you in the direction of victory?
___
___

→ Week 39: Praying for Our Children ←

As parents, we don't always know how to pray for our children. Of course, we want what is best for them, but do we really know what is best? It may have been easier to define that when they were small when we asked God to help them learn their *ABC*'s or to color within the lines. Sometimes we prayed that they wouldn't bite other kids and would learn how to wait their turn. When our daughter was younger, we were constantly praying for her to be obedient to us especially during the teen years. But as time marches on, our children face bigger issues and life becomes complicated. As a result, our prayers and knowing how best to pray becomes complicated as well.

Remember the story of Jesus immediately before His death and resurrection. He was traveling to Jerusalem with His disciples, and the mother of two of the disciples came to Him with a special request.

> *Then the mother of Zebedee's sons came with her sons, kneeling down and asking something of Him. And he said to her, "What do you wish?" She said to Him, "Grant that these two sons of mine may sit, one on your right hand and the other on the left, in Your kingdom." But Jesus answered and said, "You do not know what you ask"* (Matthew 20:20-22).

You see, at that time, this dear lady was under the impression that Jesus was about to build His kingdom on earth. Like any good mother, she wanted to make sure her sons received highly placed roles and positions of importance in His royal court. She was excited to make this request because she loved her sons and wanted them to do well in life, so her request was from the loving heart of a mother.

But Jesus knew what she didn't. He knew that He was to die an agonizing death before coming into His true kingdom, and He knew that anyone who wanted to be a part of that kingdom would have to drink from the same cup from which He was about to drink. I often wonder that had this mother understood what she was really asking for and the real implications, would she still have made the same request? Would her prayers still have been the same?

And that is a question for you and me too. As we pray for our children and ask God for what we think is best for them, have we stopped to consider that our ideas of what's best may not be best at all or may require that our children go through difficulties that we hadn't anticipated?

The Bible teaches that we are to make all our requests known to God. But we must always remember to follow Christ's example in Gethsemane when making these requests. He said, "If it is possible, let this cup pass from me; nevertheless, not as I will, but as You will" (Matthew 26:39). More than His own desires for His life, He wanted God's will for His life. And that should be our prayer too. More than wanting what we think is best for our children, we must desire God's best for them. After all, He knows what they were designed to do and has placed a divine purpose for their lives in their hearts. As their parents, we are to help them walk in their divine purpose. Only then will they have the best.

Week 39 Memory Verse

Before I formed you in your mother's womb I knew you; before you were born I sanctified you (Jeremiah 1:5).

Daily Quiet Reflections

What is one secret desire or dream that you have for your child?
___
___

How do you know if you should ask God for this?
___
___

What do you trust God to do in your child's life?
___
___

Read Isaiah 49:15, Matthew 19:13-14, and Luke 18:15. What reassurance do you receive regarding God's care and concern for you and your children?
___
___

What does the memory verse tell you about the extent of God's knowledge regarding us?
___
___

How does this reassure you that He has a plan and a destiny for your child?
___
___

↛ Week 40: Are You Waiting on an Answer or Waiting on God? ↚

We all know how difficult waiting can be. It seems as though life is full of times when we must wait—wait in line at the bank for the next teller, wait at the ice cream shop for our number to be called, or wait for the train home to come at the end of a long work day. Our opportunities to wait seem unlimited.

However, the most difficult waiting is when we must wait for an answer from God. We often pray about serious life issues and circumstances that require guidance. We go to God and ask Him to show us the way; and then we wait. What makes the waiting more difficult is that we are frequently not quite sure what method God will use to provide His answer. Will it come through a change in our circumstances? Will it be a coincidental word spoken by a wise friend? Will it come directly from His Word? Will it take hours, days, or years? We know from prior experience an answer could manifest itself in many different ways and at a time not necessarily designed by us. Before it does, we have to get through the solitary confinement of "the wait."

I was experiencing such a time recently when I desperately needed an answer from God. I called out to Him, saying, "Oh God, you know the answer; why won't You just tell me?" It was then that God redirected my attention to the Scripture that says, "Wait on the Lord. Be of good courage and He shall strengthen your heart. Wait, I say, on the Lord" (Psalm 27:14).

I noticed something about this Scripture that I had not noticed before. It says to wait on *the Lord*. The Scripture doesn't instruct us to wait on an *answer*. The instruction is very specific. We are to wait on the Lord. What's the difference? Well, think of it this way: When you are waiting on an answer, you may already have a certain outcome that you have in mind. In fact, you may even begin to look for signals or signs that suggest that the outcome you desire is in some way happening or about to happen. When circumstances don't line up with your expectations, despair begins; you may even start to lose hope.

On the other hand, when you wait on God, you begin to focus on Him and His attributes of sovereignty, faithfulness, and unfailing love. It is this focus that provides peace during the wait, strengthens you, and causes you to know in your spirit that everything will be okay. That is why the Scriptures continue to reiterate this message:

Yet the Lord longs to be gracious to you; he rises to show you compassion. For the Lord is a God of justice. Blessed are all who wait for him (Isaiah 30:18).

Be still before the Lord and wait patiently for him (Psalm 37:7).

We wait in hope for the Lord; he is our help and our shield (Psalm 33:20).

In Scriptures, we are told over and over not to wait on an answer but to wait on the Lord. The good news is that God is always with us; as we wait on Him, we know that we are not alone.

Today, if you find yourself in a season of waiting on an answer from God, change your focus. Stop waiting on an answer and begin waiting on God. You will learn, as I am learning, that God's focus is always on our relationship with Him; and He uses whatever means necessary to spend time alone with us. Sometimes, it is through the waiting that we come to recognize how precious this time alone with Him can be.

Week 40 Memory Verse

Yet the Lord longs to be gracious to you; he rises to show you compassion. For the Lord is a God of justice. Blessed are all who wait for him! (Isaiah 30:18).

Daily Quiet Reflections

Recall a time when you had to wait on the Lord. What was the most difficult part of waiting?
_____
_____

What do you think is the difference between waiting on God and waiting on an answer from God?
_____
_____

Do believe there are times when God purposefully "drags His feet" before He answers your prayer? Why or why not?
_____
_____

Read Daniel 9: 1-23. What does this tell you about one possibility of what happens in the spiritual realm when you pray?
_____
_____

How does this passage reassure you that God is listening to your prayers when you are waiting on Him?
_____
_____

What is one thing you can do to change your focus from waiting on the answer to waiting on God?
_____
_____

⇥ Week 41: The Blessings of Lingering ⇤

I don't know about you, but my life is fairly busy these days. I'm a part of the "sandwich generation," those who are still raising kids while simultaneously being a parent to elder parents. A few weeks ago, my dear father, who is in his eighties, called me on the phone. It was obvious that he was all set to have a nice long chat. But I had things to do. So I began to do what all busy people do. I tried to hurry the conversation along. I gave short answers such as, "Okay, well, I gotta go . . . "; "Sure, sure, no problem, well, I gotta go . . . "; "That's funny, Dad. Okay, well, you take care now, I gotta go . . . ." Nothing was working! He continued to talk. Finally, I gave in to the inevitable and found a chair so I could settle in for a talk with my father. We weren't talking about anything in particular. I wasn't asking for anything like in the good old days. We were just enjoying each other's company, sharing stories, laughing, and reminiscing about days gone by with little pieces of advice thrown in by my dad for good measure. Before I knew it, an entire hour had passed! Then my father said something that touched me. He said, "Daughter, I sure have enjoyed talking to you." And I said, "Me too, Dad." And I meant it.

Later while taking a walk in the park, I was going over the conversation in my head and reflecting on how good it had been to spend time with my father. I wondered why I had been so reluctant to hear all the old stories again or to simply talk about nothing at all. Then I had what I've come to recognize as a "God moment." While thinking of my earthly father, it was easy to transition to thoughts of my heavenly Father. How similar my behavior has been with Him on occasion. There have been times when I've tried to have some quiet time with God, but while flipping through my Bible, I've heard myself saying, "Oh, I've read that before"; "I've already heard that"; or "I know that lesson." In situations like these, I typically close my Bible with a little prayer and go about my day.

It occurred to me that sometimes our heavenly Father just wants to be with us in fellowship. Not because we need advice on a pressing issue. Not because we're asking for something. And not because some emergency has happened in our lives. But just as my earthly father demonstrated, sometimes God just wants us to enjoy each other's company. And God also likes to retell us the old, old stories that we've heard a million times. These would be stories of David slaying Goliath, of how Moses and the children of Israel crossed the Red Sea, or how Esther the queen helped to save her people. These stories we know by heart but they never get old from the telling. Sometimes, God wants us to share about the book we just read, or the funny incident that happened at the grocery store, or how our kitchen really needs a new floor but who can find anybody good these days to lay tile?!

God simply wants to linger in our presence and have us linger in His.

So that is what I did. I begin talking to God as I walked through the park—enjoying His company, telling my silly stories, listening with my heart for His stories, and settling in for a nice long chat. Before I knew it, we had walked four miles!

As I ended my walk in the park and headed to my car, I believe I heard Him say, "Daughter, I really enjoyed talking to you." And I replied, "Me too, Dad."

Oh, the blessing of fellowship! The wonder of lingering in His awesome presence!

If your time alone with God has become routine, limited to your prayer requests for yourself, or if you're reading the Word and find yourself thinking as I did, *Oh, I've read that story before*, take time out to linger with God. Find a place where you can sense His presence. He will meet you there. And you may find, as I did, that your time together will have you coming back for more.

Week 41 Memory Verse

Yes, all the things I once thought were so important are gone from my life. Compared to the high privilege of knowing Christ Jesus as my Master, firsthand, everything I once thought I had going for me is insignificant . . . I've dumped it all in the trash so that I could embrace Christ and be embraced by him. I didn't want some petty, inferior brand of righteousness that comes from keeping a list of rules when I could get the robust kind that comes from trusting Christ—God's righteousness . . . I gave up all that inferior stuff so I could know Christ personally, experience his resurrection power . . . (Philippians 3:8-10 MSG).

Daily Quiet Reflections

What is one thing that keeps you from lingering in God's presence and getting to know Him better?

If you do not sense the love of God for you, what can you do to come to know the realities of His love for you and His desire to spend time with you?

Is there ever a time when you are out of God's reach?

What is the most important thing you have learned about yourself and God while in His presence?

How does that affect your future relationship with Him?

Read this week's memory verse again. What is the Apostle Paul throwing out in his life and why was this important to him?
_____
_____

What do you need to toss out of your life in order to make God a priority in it?
_____
_____

→ Week 42: Struggling To Obey ←

When I was pregnant with our daughter, I had severe morning sickness during the first trimester. I was miserable. I was not only sick in the morning, but I was also nauseous all day, not vomiting, but constantly feeling as though I would at any moment. Those three months were tough!

I remember the day I discovered some relief.

My husband had been saying I needed something to eat because I was avoiding food since the sight of it made me sick. He kept insisting that I needed the nourishment and so did the baby. I wanted to smack him for being right, but instead I told him to bring me some dry toast. I cautiously nibbled on it, thinking any minute that I would have a problem. However, a remarkable thing occurred! The more toast I ate, the less nauseated I felt! I was not completely out of the woods, but clearly well enough to get up, get dressed, and go to work that day.

I soon discovered that if I nibbled on some crackers or toast or something throughout the day, the nausea abated. In fact, it became apparent that keeping my stomach from being completely empty was the remedy for my morning sickness. I realize now that a spiritual principle was at work as well. We are frequently miserable in our circumstances. We find ourselves sick with worry and anxiety, wondering what the next day will bring. This may even keep us from reading God's Word and desiring to obey it. But God's Word is exactly what we need during times of trouble. We may think, *How can I praise Him and give Him thanks when my situation is so bad?*

Everything within us wants to reject the only food that will nourish our souls and take away the queasiness of worry. Many times we prefer to wallow in our struggle to fix the situation ourselves, only to feel weaker and weaker as we refuse to submit to the power of God's Word. My experience is that God is relentless. He will not stop until we surrender. Day and night we will sense His quiet voice saying, "This is the path, walk in it." When we finally take that step in the direction of God's Word, He moves in like a flood with power to enable us to make the next step and then the next. Before we realize it, we are walking in the truth of God's Word as we read it, meditate on it, and obey what He tells us to do.

Not long ago, while having this very same struggle, I decided to write about the struggle and the ultimate victory that comes when we decide to obey.

Struggling To Obey

Today is such a lovely day,
The world looks bright, so clear the way.
There is one thing I want to say,
"O Lord, I wish I could obey."
It started with a choice to make,
To have my rights for my own sake.
But then the other was less fair,
And yet God seemed to draw me there.
The civil war began that day,
"O Lord, I wish I could obey."

On I struggled deep within,
It wasn't clear which side would win.
One day—my rights! And then—no way!
The battle raged day after day.
My soul so tired and still I say,
"O Lord, I wish I could obey."

The fear, the turmoil of giving in,
But yet my flesh still wants to win.
Maybe a compromise would save the day?
"O Lord, I wish I could obey."

No power left, no peace is found,
The urge to lay my weapons down.

But there's an enemy that has me bound,
I can't look up, I can't turn 'round.
With my small voice I finally say,
"O Lord please help me to obey."

I wait for rescue; I hope for grace,
I want the kindness of His face.
Is He still with me? Doubt brings dismay
My enemy smiles, "You can't obey!"
But then His power, I hear Him say,
"Let go! Unbind! Move out of My way!"
My enemy flees, I joyfully say,
"O Lord, you taught me to obey!"

Week 42 Memory Verse

*Lord, we show our **trust** in you by **obey**ing your laws; our heart's desire is to glorify your name* (Isaiah 26:8, emphasis added).

Daily Quiet Reflections

Recall a time when you struggled to obey God. What made it so difficult to be obedient?
___
___

How did God help you during the struggle?
___
___

What are some lessons that you have learned from disobedience?
___
___

What have been the results to obedience to God in the past?
___
___

What do you think is the secret to have a heart eager to obey God?
___
___

What part does trust play in creating a desire to be obedient to God?
___
___

→ Week 43: Destinations ←

One of my favorite times of year is Easter! Besides the obvious reasons that I love this season, I always take time to reflect on the true meaning of Easter. The fact that God, the Creator, would come to the earth in the person of Jesus Christ is still something that fills me with wonder and gratitude. I always think of the reason He came—to make a way for you and me to one day return to the place where it all began and live eternally with Him.

Whenever I think about this, I am reminded that we are all on a journey now, the journey of our lives. As with any trip, we all have to make preparations for our destination. Sometimes the most difficult part of the journey is choosing where to go. Our family found this to be true in trying to plan a simple family reunion. With over forty people involved, finding a venue that everyone could agree upon was a challenge. We decided on a cruise but then had to decide which cruise to take. Emails floated back and forth as we discussed price ranges, length of the cruise, cruise ships, schedules, and finally choosing a departure date. And that's where we hit a roadblock. We never could find a date that would work for all of us. Despite all our preparation, that was the one detail on which we could never settle, so we never even left the shore. I wonder what adventures we missed, what fun times were lost, and what memories were never made.

Our journey here on earth is already settled. We will live and then we will die. But for many of us, one detail still remains: What is my destination? Where will I end up after I die? What preparation have I made while here on earth to spend eternity with God? Have I accepted the free ticket, the free gift offered through Jesus Christ? And if not, what adventures will I miss, what fun times will be lost, and what memories with God will never be made because I chose to live apart from Him eternally? These are sobering questions for such a sacred time of year.

During the next Easter season, as you celebrate an event that occurred over two thousand years ago, the Resurrection of Christ, the

Messiah, choose to remember the reason for the season. And then be sure of your destination. Before you know it, your time on earth will be gone. God sent Jesus so He could welcome you home!

Week 43 Memory Verse

For God so loved the world, that He gave His one and only Son. That whoever believes in Him shall not perish but have eternal life (John 3:16).

Daily Quiet Reflections

What do you think heaven will be like?
___
___

Where do you believe that you will spend eternity?
___

Are you sure of your future in eternity? Explain your answer.
___
___

How can you be certain that you will spend eternity with God?
___

What does the Resurrection of Christ mean to you?
___
___

Read the book of John for God's complete revelation on arriving safely home. If you are not certain of your destination, pray and ask God to reveal truth to you in this area.

⇾ Week 44: Are You Living Greatly? ⇽

While dining at a favorite salad bar, we sat next to a family that had an adorable little girl. She couldn't have been more than three or four, and she was as cute as a button. At one point during the meal, she collapsed into a fit of giggles. Her delight was contagious, and soon we were laughing too. We learned from her mother that the little girl was relishing the fact that she had "stolen" her aunt's seat at the table while her aunt was making a trip to the salad bar. When her aunt returned to find her small niece sitting in her chair, she immediately entered into the spirit of the game, putting a pretend scowl on her face and exclaiming, "What happened to my seat?"

The little girl responded with a burst of giggles again. We all began to laugh as the aunt and niece chatted back and forth over whose seat it really was. All of this stopped, however, when the little girl noticed that her aunt had brought back a piece of pie from the dessert bar. She immediately lost interest in the stolen chair game and grabbed the pie right out of her aunt's hands. The look on her aunt's face was one of amused astonishment as if to say, "First you take my chair, and now you have my pie!" She smiled at the precocious child and willingly give her the pie too.

Later as I reflected on that scene, I thought of something Jesus said when He was asked by His followers, "Which of us is the greatest in the kingdom of heaven?" Jesus called a small child over to Him and put the child among them. Then He said,

I assure you, unless you turn from your sins and become as little children, you will never get into the kingdom of heaven. Therefore, anyone who becomes as humble as this little child is the greatest in the kingdom of heaven (Matthew 18:1-4).

I thought about what it meant to become like that innocent little girl I had seen at the restaurant, absolutely without a worry or care. She trusted that her parents would take care of her, believed that her world was a safe place, and counted on each day to be filled with people like her aunt and delicious pieces of pie. Unless one accepts the absolute goodness, faithfulness, and love of God, this would be a formidable task. Resting securely in Him just as that little girl rested in the security of her parents' care is tantamount to achieving greatness in God's economy. Why? Because by relying on God completely, we rely on the greatest One.

I know that little girl had days that probably were not so much fun. I'm sure she had her share of tummy aches and scraped knees. She may have even experienced sorrow in her young life that caused her to run to her parents in tears. But I have a feeling that even during her childhood woes, she still rested in the care of her parents, knowing they would make everything all better.

I have a feeling that's what Jesus was saying to His disciples and ultimately to each of us. When we learn to rest and hope in God no matter what, we are exactly where we need to be to experience how truly great God is and to experience that greatness lived out in our own lives just as it should be.

Week 44 Memory Verse

*Then he said, "I tell you the truth, unless you turn from your sins and become like **little children**, you will never get into the kingdom of heaven"* (Matthew 18:3, emphasis added).

Daily Quiet Reflections

What does it mean to become like little children?
___
___

Why do you think this is important to God?
___
___

What truth about Christ causes us to turn away from our sins, repent, and accept Him into our hearts and lives?
___
___

Does love have anything to do with your destiny?
___
___

If you do not sense the love of God, what can you do to come to know the realities of His love?
___
___

Read 1 John 1:9. What assurance do you receive about God's willingness to forgive your sins?
___
___

➸ Week 45: A Homecoming ☙

A former Miss USA just happens to be a friend of my daughter's. One weekend during her reign, a homecoming was planned to celebrate her return to her home state after winning the coveted national title. It was exciting to be a part of welcoming her back home. Everyone wanted to take a picture with her, friends and sponsors were there to wish her well, and the air was filled with joy and celebration! An abundance of food, music, cake, and flowers comprised a homecoming fit for a queen. Think about all the homecomings that have occurred over time, from war heroes to those held hostage. Joy overflows when seeing a beloved one who was once very far away. Happiness cascades in the hearts of moms and dads, brothers and sisters, friends and loved ones.

The Bible describes a similar scene in Luke 15. Jesus used this story of the prodigal son as an illustration of God's love for us. He wanted to demonstrate that we have all been far away from home, but God's greatest desire is our homecoming—when we return to a right relationship with Him. As each one of God's own children return to Him, I can only imagine the great celebration that must occur in heaven. How the angels must rejoice, the heavenly band strikes up a chord, the singing begins, and the joy and celebration ensues for one once lost but now found. You can almost hear our Father, the God of the universe, saying, "Welcome home, darling child!"

Yes, we celebrated that weekend, admiring our beautiful queen and her lovely crown, wishing her well as she went on to compete for the title of Miss Universe. Our hearts were indeed merry because one of our own was home. In like fashion, a day will come when there will be a homecoming, a great celebration. I don't want to miss this celebration! The host is Jesus, and all are invited to come. I have already made plans to be there. What about you?

Week 45 Memory Verse

But when he was still a great way off, his father saw him and had compassion, and ran and fell on his neck and kissed him . . . the father said to his servants, "Bring out the best robe and put it on him, and put a ring on his hand and sandals on his feet. And bring the fatted calf here and kill it, and let us eat and be merry; for this my son was dead and is alive again; he was lost and is found." And they began to be merry (Luke 15:20,22-24 NIV).

Daily Quiet Reflections

Read the story of the prodigal son found in Luke 15:11-32. With what part of the story do you most identify?

_____
_____

What are some of the attributes of the father in the story that are also a description of God?

_____
_____

Why do you think the father in the story was so willing to accept his wayward son back home?

_____
_____

What would be the perfect ending to your life story?

_____
_____

The prodigal son thought he knew how is life should end too. How can you guard yourself from hoping for a life that may not be best for you?

_____
_____

Read Jeremiah 29:11-13. What assurance do you receive that God has already written a perfect ending to your life story?

_____
_____

⇾ Week 46: I've Got You Covered! ⇽

During the news coverage of a recent election primary, I was very amused when some of the national news anchors were attempting to figure out what caption should go under a picture of a candidate and his wife who were celebrating his nomination. She was giving him a thumbs up in victory. One caller from the audience suggested that the candidate's wife seemed to be saying, "I've got your back, Boo." The news anchors weren't sure what "Boo" meant and learned from the caller that it was the new term of endearment that is presently being used by many, similar to "Honey" or "Sweetie," which were popular during the 1950s. My husband and I have used the term "Boo" in our family for years, so we thought it was quite comical that these well-traveled news people were limited in their knowledge of the present day love language.

Later when having some quiet time, I was praying about concerns I had for the future, putting into practice my belief that we should take all our cares to our heavenly Father because He cares about us. During this time of prayer, I opened my Bible to Hebrews 13:5 (AMP) and read the following:

Let your character or moral disposition be free from love of money [including greed, avarice, lust, and craving for earthly possessions] and be satisfied with your present [circumstances and with what you have]; for He [God] Himself has said, I will not in anyway fail you nor give you up nor leave you without support. I will not in any degree leave you helpless nor forsake nor let you down (relax my hold on you)! [Assuredly not!]

That was so reassuring to me! In fact, as I broke this Scripture down into sections, I realized that God is saying seven key messages through this passage.

1. He will not fail us in any way.
2. He will not give us up.

3. He will not leave us without support.
4. He will not leave us helpless.
5. He will not forsake us.
6. He will not let us down.
7. He will not relax his hold on us.

In other words, He is saying, "I've got your back, Boo!" I don't know about you, but that makes me want to rejoice! So if you are having one of those days where you are tempted to worry or fret, don't be anxious! Instead, be encouraged by the message from God's Word: He's got your back, Boo!

Week 46 Memory Verse

*And I will ask the Father, and he will give you another Advocate, who will **never leave you** (John 14:16, emphasis added).*

Daily Quiet Reflections

Read the memory verse for this week again. Jesus makes a promise and refers to an Advocate. Who is the Advocate? (Hint: see John 14:26.)
_____
_____

According to John 14:26, what is one role of the Holy Spirit in the life of the believer?
_____
_____

Read Psalm 91:7-14. According to verses 11 and 14, whom will God use to ensure your protection?
_____
_____

What must you do to be sure that you are walking in the protection of God? (Hint: see Psalm 91:9-10.)
_____
_____

How do these promises help you to feel secure in Christ?
_____
_____

Spend time in prayer, thanking Him for all the ways He takes care of you.

→ WEEK 47: WHAT SEASON IS IT NOW? ←

A good friend of mine and I are accountability partners in attempting to break some bad habits. We agreed to get our assignments to each other by 3:30 p.m. each day and found ourselves missing the deadline every time. At one point she laughingly said, "Well it's 3:30 somewhere in the world!" I completely agreed!

I applied that same principle while studying a passage of Scripture in which Jesus said to His disciples,

> *Do you not say, It is still four months until harvest time comes? Look! I tell you, raise your eyes and observe the fields and see how they are already white for harvesting* (John 4:35 AMP).

An analogy was being used in this passage to help the disciples know what time it really was! While they were waiting until the right time to begin their work, He was saying, "The time is now!"

In agriculture, the harvest is the process of gathering mature crops from the field. Before the sixteenth century, *harvest* was the term usually used to refer to the autumn season, a time where most farmers celebrated the joyful time of finally being able to gather their crops. And yet today, many crops are gathered at various times during the year. In fact, depending on what part of the world you live in—to use my friend's expression—on any given day, "It's probably harvest time somewhere in the world!"

And that is the point. Is it harvest time in your life? Could it be that sowing has already occurred, and the time spent waiting is now finished? Is it time to harvest the fruit from seed already planted in your life? Is it possible there are relationships ready for harvest? Or maybe it is an opportunity that you have been longing for and now presents itself; is fear keeping you from the harvest? Or as the Scripture points out, are there people in your life who are ready for harvest and only need someone like you to guide the way?

Whatever your answer may be, know this: at any given time, God has already provided a harvest. He is waiting for someone to reap it. Could that someone be you?

Week 47 Memory Verse

Thus the saying "One sows and another reaps" is true. I sent you to reap (harvest) what you have not worked for. Others have done the hard work, and you have reaped the benefits of their labor" (John 4:37-38).

Daily Quiet Reflections:

How can you know which season of life you are in—sowing, planting, or reaping?

What are some opportunities that might provide you with some idea that you may be stepping into a new season?

Why do you believe that it is so important to God that we reap the harvest?

What would be an indication of harvest in your life today?

If you could see your place in the lives of others the way God sees your place, what would you see?

How might God be glorified if others viewed you as the harvest in their lives?

➤ Week 48: Praise After the Storm ✦

The area of the country that I live in recently sustained a hurricane. The storm left our community some time ago, but its effect is still very present as people try to return to their lives. That is easier for some than others. As a result, writing has been difficult for me because like many others, I have been so distracted with all it takes to put my life together again after something unexpected (and unwanted) happens.

In my quiet time, I asked God to show me how I could bless Him now that the storm is past, and He reminded me that sometimes—when we least feel like it—that is the time for worship. And so I do. I worship God for His ultimate protection in the storm and for His strength for the days ahead. Let the promises of His Word be a prayer that you speak no matter what difficulty you may find yourself in today. Despite our circumstances, God's Word remains true today and forever.

> *For God watches over the way of the righteous* (Psalm 1:6).
> *Blessed are all that take refuge in Him* (Psalm 2:12).
> *From the Lord comes deliverance* (Psalm 3:8).
> *Know that the Lord has set apart the godly for Himself* (Psalm 4:3).
> *For surely, O Lord, you bless the righteous; you surround them*
> *with your favor as with a shield* (Psalm 5:12).
> *The Lord accepts my prayer. All my enemies will be ashamed*
> *and dismayed; they will turn back in sudden disgrace*
> (Psalm 6:9-10).
> *My shield is God Most High* (Psalm 7:10).
> *For You have never forsaken those who seek you* (Psalm 9:10).
> *The Lord is King for ever and ever* (Psalm 10:16).
> *But I trust in Your unfailing Love* (Psalm 13:5).
> *For God is present in the company of the righteous* (Psalm 14:5).
> *Lord, you have assigned me my portion and my cup;*
> *you have made my lot secure* (Psalm 16:5).

Week 48 Memory Verse

O Lord, you will keep me safe and protect me (Psalm 12:7).

Daily Quiet Reflections

Why is it difficult to praise God in the middle of our tough circumstances?
_____
_____

Of the passages quoted in this week's inspiration, which gives you the most comfort and why?
_____
_____

What is faith when it is translated into day-to-day living?
_____
_____

How does faith help us to praise God despite our circumstances?
_____
_____

Read Hebrews 11:6. What do you learn from this passage about faith?
_____
_____

Read Ephesians 1:13-15. What are some reasons given that should provoke our praise?
_____
_____

⇾ Week 49: Second Chances ⇽

While visiting home during a break, our daughter learned the realities of living on a budget. We have always encouraged her to spend her money wisely and take care of her financial responsibilities first before buying something she wants. While shopping at a favorite store during this break, she spotted a pair of designer jeans she just could not overlook. She wondered aloud if she could afford them, and I reminded her that she had her tithe, rent, and utilities money to set aside. I observed her making mental calculations before announcing proudly, "Yes, I think I can still afford this!" A grin of satisfaction crossed her face as she made her purchase.

Later, as we talked about her purchase, I inquired about her ability to buy groceries for the rest of the month. She blithely replied, "I still have thirty dollars in my account." I laughingly responded, "And you think thirty dollars is going to buy groceries for two weeks? Darling, you obviously plan to live on peanut butter and crackers!" Needless to say, she was not amused but was too proud to let on that she too was slightly concerned about how she would survive with such a small amount of cash.

The next day, as she was preparing to return to school, I mentioned that we had an abundance of deli meats and cheeses left over from a reception that we had hosted the day before. The words were barely out of my mouth before she squealed, "God truly does provide! My very own manna and quail!" (Of course she was referring to the heavenly food God sent to Moses and the children of Israel during the great Exodus in the Bible). I couldn't help but laugh. She had clearly been praying about her lack of money and her need for groceries! She viewed those leftovers as God's provision in her time of need. With that, we packed a cooler, and she took her "manna and quail" back to school.

I reflected on how often God bails us out even when we make unwise decisions. This is an example of His grace or unmerited favor towards us. Why does He do it? Because He loves us and remembers that we are only clay. And thank God He does! Which of us hasn't done something like spent our grocery money on jeans? Or chose a good path rather than the best path? Even still, we experience His patience as He corrects us and guides us back as only the God of second chances can do.

I have a feeling that after my girl has her fill of "manna and quail," she'll think twice before spending her grocery money on another pair of jeans. But more importantly, she will know firsthand how to choose the best path next time. Isn't this how we grow up in life?

We must also mature spiritually as we journey through life. Sometimes we choose wisely and other times not. We may never walk perfectly, but we can walk victoriously when we choose to follow God. And as we do, the truth of Romans 8:28 will become evident in our lives.

Week 49 Memory Verse

That's why we can be sure that every detail in our lives of love for God is worked into something good (Romans 8:28 MSG).

Daily Quiet Reflections

What are some lessons you have learned as a result of choices that you made in the past?
_____
_____

What do you now do differently as a result of these lessons learned?
_____
_____

Looking at your life, can you remember purposefully seeking the path God has for you?
_____
_____

Read Jeremiah 29:11-13. What are three things you can be assured of based on the truth in this passage?
_____
_____

Since God has a plan for your life, how does He handle bad choices you may have made in the past? (Hint: Meditate on Romans 8:28 for the answer.)
_____
_____

How does the truth found in Romans 8:28 help you to move into the future with confidence?
_____
_____

⇢ Week 50: What Would You Do If You Really Believed God? ⇠

One day when faced with a difficult challenge, I asked myself, *What would you do if you really believed God?* This question took me by surprise because anyone who knows me knows I believe God. So I was startled when this question just popped up in my mind. Hmmm.

As a student of psychology, I immediately knew I needed to delve into the meaning of this question. Could it possibly mean the same thing as, *What would you do if you were not afraid?* Somehow, I knew it went deeper than that. Because the true test of faith is not whether or not you are afraid. The true test is your willingness to take action even when your knees are shaking and you don't know the outcome.

I surmised that the real question was not only the one being asked but was actually a series of questions such as,

• What would you do if you really believed God is sovereign and has this challenging circumstance under control?

• What would you do if you believed God will work everything out for good even if you can't see how right now?

• What would you do if you really believed God could take any mistake you make along the way and use it to bring you up higher in character, while keeping the mistake from causing you to miss your destiny?

• What would you do if you believed God really does keep His Word?

Approaching the topic from this viewpoint, I knew that if I really believed all those things about God, I'd do whatever was necessary to go out on that limb with Him! The challenge that had me stumped initially took on a new meaning. The challenge was not the circumstance. Instead, it was making the decision to believe God—again. Why again? Because I know that this will not be the last time I will ask myself this question.

There will always be more challenges and in some cases, I may collapse under my own fear. But I'm very optimistic. The more I practice believing God, the more I do. The more I do, the more opportunities I get to believe Him again.

What about you? If faced with a challenging decision today, ask yourself, *What would I do if I really believed God?* As you keep believing God, you will find His faithfulness will cause you to continue.

Week 50 Memory Verse

Because of the Lord's great love we are not consumed, for his compassions never fail. They are new every morning; great is your faithfulness (Lamentations 3:22-23).

Daily Quiet Reflections

What is the difference between believing God versus believing in God?

___

Why is it so easy to confuse believing in God with believing God?

___

How can knowing this distinction make a difference in how you conduct your life?

___

Read Hebrews 11:6. Based on this passage, why is it important for us to not only believe in God but also to believe God?

___

What does this passage say God is faithful to do when we diligently seek Him?

___

What is something that you need to believe God about today? Pray that God will increase your faith to believe what He says and to be obedient to His Word.

___

→ Week 51: A Better Vantage Point ←

The other day, my daughter was driving me to the airport. She was on a holiday break and decided to take a route that would cause us to go by her old high school campus. As we passed the school, I asked her, "Does it look small to you now?" She replied, "It sure does! I can't believe I once thought it was so big! When I was in high school, I used to worry that I wouldn't be able to find my classes because there were more buildings than when I was in elementary school!"

Of course, now that she is at a university with a campus that stretches out for miles, her perspective has completely changed. She sees her old campus in a new light and from a different vantage point. Likewise, when we look back on situations in our lives that seemed huge at the time, and we made it through by the grace of God, we too wonder, *Why did I think that was such a huge problem? It all worked out in the end, and I survived.* Sometimes we need to step into another vantage point in order to obtain a true perspective. Sometimes we need to get God's vantage point to realize it is all small stuff to Him.

One of my favorite passages of Scripture is found in Jeremiah 33:3, which says, *"Call to me and I will answer you and show you great and mighty things that you do not know."* Very often, we don't even know what we don't know, but it is good to realize that God always does. When facing overwhelming odds, a bad economy, a setback in a relationship, or when your vantage point is at the bottom of the mountain, call on God. He can bring you up to His vantage point above the mountain. Then you will see what is on the other side and have the insider's track on those great and mighty things that you did not know. Now, isn't that good news?

Week 51 Memory Verse

Call to me and I will answer you and show you great and mighty things that you do not know (Jeremiah 33:3).

Daily Quiet Reflections

What happens in your life when you do not talk to God?
_____
_____

What happens in your life when you lose sight of God's goals for you?
_____
_____

In this week's memory verse, God promises that if you call on Him, He will answer you and show you things you do not know. What does this tell you about the importance of having a consistent prayer life?
_____
_____

Read Daniel 10: 10-14. Based on this passage, what happened that caused a delay in Daniel receiving God's answer to his prayer?
_____
_____

Sometimes we do not receive an immediate answer to our prayers to God; however, God promises to answer us. What instructions do we receive from Matthew 7:7 when it doesn't appear that God has answered our prayers?
_____
_____

Why is having faith critical in believing God when He says He will answer when you call on Him?
_____
_____

✧ Week 52: The Challenge ✧

The holiday season is here again, and with it comes the smells and sounds of Christmas. This is absolutely my favorite time of year, as I know is true for many of you. However, recently a series of events caused me to shift focus to the true meaning of Christmas and to begin thinking about the new year to come.

One of my daughter's schoolmates died tragically just before the Thanksgiving holiday. It was shocking and dreadful for us, but I could only imagine how sad and overwhelming it was for the parents of this beautiful child. Because of this event, I have been spending a tremendous amount of time interceding in prayer on behalf of this family, knowing that they have fallen into the depths of despair.

While praying, God impressed on my heart that the sadness I have been feeling when I think of the gravity of losing a child is small compared to the sadness He feels every time one of His own is lost to Him forever without ever coming to know Him. It made me realize that whenever we celebrate Christmas, God is reminded of His great gift of His Son and the many people that have never come into a saving knowledge of Jesus, the Messiah.

As a result, I determined right then and there that the new year would be a year of more boldness in my life, a boldness to declare who Jesus is and why I believe that He is the true Messiah who came to provide the path for us back to God. And I want to challenge you to do the same.

My challenge is this: If you do not believe in God or don't know who He is, then ask Him to show you that He is real and that He wants you to know Him and have a right relationship with Him. I believe that God will send people across your path and will allow circumstances to occur that will amaze you as you seek the truth about Him. And if you do know God through His Son Jesus Christ, then ask Him to empower you to tell what He has meant in your life to all your family and friends and to share with them why you believe that Jesus is who He says He is—the divine Son of God.

There is a popular television commercial that says, "Friends don't let friends drive drunk." I would like to amend that to say, "Friends don't let friends and others they love go through life without telling them about Jesus."

Will you take the challenge? A great deal is riding on your answer.

Week 52 Memory Verse

This is how much God loved the world: He gave his Son, his one and only Son. And this is why: so that no one need be destroyed; by believing in him, anyone can have a whole and lasting life. God didn't go to all the trouble of sending his Son merely to point an accusing finger, telling the world how bad it was. He came to help, to put the world right again. Anyone who trusts in him is acquitted; anyone who refuses to trust him has long since been under the death sentence without knowing it. And why? Because of that person's failure to believe in the one-of-a-kind Son of God when introduced to him (John 3:16-17 MSG).

Daily Quiet Reflections:

During the Christmas season, what does all the tinsel, trimming, and festivities mean to God?

_____

_____

During the Christmas season, what can you do to reach out to those people who do not understand the true meaning of Christmas?

_____

_____

How can you give a gift that truly shows, without a doubt, the wonderful love of God?

_____

_____

Read Isaiah 43:7. Based on this Scripture, what is your ultimate purpose in life?

_____

_____

How can you bring glory to God by touching others for Christ?

_____

_____

What battles can you anticipate by sharing the gospel (good news) about Christ?
_____
_____

About the Author

A sought-after life coach and speaker, Mary Banks is the author of *Living by Faith 9 to 5* and *The Multi-Faceted Woman*, both also published by Evergreen Press. A professional certified leadership and life coach, Mary coaches entrepreneurs and professionals who are seeking a more purposeful path. She is the founder of W.O.W. Consulting Group, a firm focused on leadership development, strategic planning, teambuilding, and conflict resolution in the workplace. Formerly a human resources executive in the financial services industry for more than twenty years, Mary's mission is to help connect her clients to their life purpose, empowering them to realize the divine plan and purpose for their lives. She and her husband, Melvin, and their daughter live in Houston, Texas.

To contact Mary for consultations or speaking engagements, e-mail her at:

Mary Banks
W.O.W. Consulting Group
Mary_Banks@wowconsultinggroup.com
More information is available at www.wowconsultinggroup.com
or phone: 281-537-5959

See www.maryebanks.org for information on speaking topics.